Love Thy Neighbor:

The True, Encouraging, and Hilarious Tales of a Christian Living in a Muslim Land

Alice Crocker

THE FIG & THE VINE
PUBLISHING, LLC

ACKNOWLEDGEMENTS

To the Lord God Almighty, Creator of heaven and earth, for life, health, and opportunity to complete this meager offering, designed to highlight how delightful it is to follow You.

To the lovely people of Indonesia, particularly my loved ones in Aceh, who have shown me kindness to exceed even the most glowing reputation of Asian hospitality

To Leny Katan: for being the first one to seriously suggest that I should write a book. Perhaps I have veered from your initial intent, or broadened the scope of the vision, but I thank you for pushing me to write more purposefully and for believing in me. If there is any translation to be done in the future, I do hope you will do the honors.

Mary O. Fersner: for not only recommending that I consider joining a writers' group, but for finding and escorting me to the Seacoast Writers' Group; then reading my first few stories, and declaring, "Go for the book. The world needs to hear this message." I will never forget your enthusiasm and excitement on my behalf as we've seen this book come to fruition.

To Mom and Dad: even though I came home ostensibly to serve you, you allowed me ample time and support to write, print, and reprint, all without one word of question or concern over my exorbitant use of time and materials. I thank you, too, for laughing while reading this book yourselves. I had great satisfaction in your joy while reading the manuscript. Most of all, thank you for raising us with laughter.

To my sister, Mary Crocker Cook, "Bea": for your example of courage and diligence to make continuous meaningful contribution to society. Your support has always meant the world to me, and being ridiculous with you is the best!

To the Seacoast Writers' Group, of which the late Fred Robinson and Irene Lofton were beloved members: for giggling over and making edifying remarks about my silly tales. Thank you for your immeasurable kindness to this newbie, receiving me into your fellowship, and making known valuable resources to help me along the way.

To Hilary Yeo: for your enthusiastic support and generosity with your superior and experienced editing skills to give me confidence in my silly stories. Love the Yeos!

To Judy Gladwell: for your constant encouragement, sending me resources to make me feel like publishing a book could honestly become a reality.

TABLE OF CONTENTS

In the Beginning...

The "end of the earth" was the last place I ever thought I would find myself. I never had much wanderlust or desire for adventure. I was just a simple person trying to live a decent life. A life that honored the Lord by participating in the local church and making some sort of positive contribution to society. I had no real preference of a place to live because my family moved every three years when I was growing up. We went from Virginia to Hawaii, from there to New Jersey, and on to California, and then I went to college in North Carolina before living out west as a young adult. So really, one place was as good as another as far as I was concerned. I had observed that people are people everywhere: most benign, some delightful, others challenging, a few best avoided. I discovered that there were friends to be made everywhere, largely depending on my own attitude and behavior.

My eyes began to open to the world while I was living in Texas in my late twenties. I taught English as a Second Language (ESL) on the University of Texas, Arlington campus and had students from all over the world including Thailand, France, Korea, Brazil, and Jordan. The more I got to know my students, the more I saw that language was only one of many struggles they faced when adjusting to life in

America. One Korean graduate student had been a highly respected teacher in her land, but had been derided on the UTA campus by some twenty year old in an orange vest because of a parking violation. She cried tears of rage and humiliation. A civil engineer from Jordan decried the narrow, *individual* oriented focus of American students, which resulted in them only knowing about their own, specific field of study. She and her husband had come to this country to find the American dream, but instead found convoluted bureaucracy and grave disappointment. Neither of these students, nor any other I met, expressed dislike for America. They all agreed that Americans are generally friendly and helpful, and that the freedom of expression we enjoy here was refreshing. None were sorry they came. They simply had frustrations in adjusting, i.e. culture shock.

Although my heart stirred with compassion for these students, I had no way to truly empathize with them. I had never lived outside American borders. People within America speak of major differences between the North and South, the East and West, but the differences I had experienced living in those environments were minor inconveniences compared to the trials of acclimating to a new country with different language, food, weather, and customs.

One way I hoped to become a more understanding and effective ESL teacher was to take a two year assignment in another country. When I searched the myriad of job opportunities around the world teaching English, I finally decided on a job in Indonesia. Of course, I had to get a world map to find Indonesia because I didn't know anything about it. My father knew exactly where it was and asked if I didn't want to live somewhere further away, like the moon, because Indonesia is exactly the opposite side of the world from America. If you fly to Indonesia and pass it, you're on your way home. My student from Jordan cautioned me against going to Indonesia.

"They are mostly Muslims there and they'll hate you!" Asma warned.

I found that odd because Asma herself was a Muslim and we were close friends. So I did some research and learned that Indonesia accepts five major religions and Christianity is one of them, so it wouldn't be *illegal* to be a Christian. What would be illegal would be trying to force Muslims to embrace my religion. As long as I didn't break into sermons on street corners or hand out Gospel tracts in the market, I shouldn't have any trouble. I could certainly live there as a Christian without any fear of recrimination. I would never have to deny what I believed, nor hide my Bible, and if I lived in a city that had churches, I could attend. I could even have open discussions about faith with curious neighbors as long as I didn't pressure them to change their religion. No problem! And every resource about Indonesia emphasized the outstanding hospitality of Indonesian people towards guests.

Within six months of accepting the job, I was on my way to Indonesia. And that's where my adventure begins. After my initial two year contract, I came home for six months and returned for another three year contract, and then another, and another, totaling eleven splendid years in Indonesia, mostly on the island of Sumatra. I would love to return for another twenty or thirty years!

In August of 2004, my dear friend Leny Katan said to

me,

"Alice, many foreigners come to Indonesia and have to begin from scratch as they adjust to this culture. You have assimilated well and love it here. You really should write a book to help others."

I liked the idea and began to think about lessons I could share with newcomers to ease their transition, to comfort them during the heavy culture shock days, or just give them a giggle and remind them not take themselves too seriously. But the tsunami that devastated our beloved province, Aceh, in December of that year interrupted all our lives, and everything else was pushed to the background. So here I sit, five years later, reviving a dream. Do I have valuable lessons to share, or just silly stories? Lord willing, both.

I hope these stories, all true, will encourage readers to: a.) fully entrust their lives to God, because a joyous adventure awaits, and b.) open their hearts to people who are "foreign" and see individuals, not stereotypes; because in the scope of creation and journeying through this temporary world with all its joy and promise, struggle and uncertainty, we are all in this together.

1

An Auspicious Start

I might have known that my life in Indonesia would be a wild, glorious adventure with constant transition between comic tension (read *panic*) and cathartic relief when my initial entry into the country on June 20, 1997 began with such suspense. Flying alone, at 31 years old, with a background in business, I was committed to making a good first impression on my new boss. I imagined that I would glide off the plane professionally dressed with not a hair out of place, and extend my hand for a warm yet confident greeting that would establish from the start, "You won't be sorry I'm on your team."

I wore pantyhose and pumps for my 30 hour journey of being stuffed into an economy class airline seat. I knew those pantyhose were a mistake long before we even hit the Pacific, but they completed *the look*, and that's what I was after — to get off to a strong start on my new career as an English teacher overseas. After brief stops in Los Angeles and Taipei, we landed in Jakarta sometime in the afternoon, which was the middle of the night to my cramped, totally disheveled self.

I was not discouraged, however. No, I was greatly relieved that the pressure cooker trip was behind me. I wouldn't be popping home for Christmas and Easter, though, that was for sure. I had no intention of taking a flight longer than three hours for at least two years, when I'd be at the end of my contract and on my way home.

With renewed enthusiasm and a smile plastered across my face, I gathered my two 70 pound bags and headed to the arrival hall, where I would meet my new boss and begin my new life. The first thing I noticed was that, almost without exception, I was larger than everyone in there. And while there were *some* Caucasians, there weren't many. "Ah… all the better for me," I thought, "my boss and I will be able to recognize each other right away." My eyes began to search, roaming to and fro throughout the arrival hall, certain that at any moment I would make eye contact with the American man I would so impress with my professionalism.

Looking… looking… eyes roving… roving… body turning slowly to scour every corner of the arrival area… The crowd began to thin. Perhaps a more spiritually mature person would have taken a moment to pray, asking for assistance, but I had decided it was time to take more aggressive measures. In my infinite wisdom, I determined that the best strategy would be to focus on each Caucasian male in his 40's or 50's and wave my arms to get his attention. Then, upon eye contact, I would lift my eyebrows, gesture to myself, and clearly mouth the words, "Are you looking for ME?" with a reassuring nod.

Figuring this was a fool proof plan, I began the pursuit and, one after the other, I would get the same disturbed look from my would be knight in shining armor: his eyes would open wide, he'd shake his head vigorously "NO," then furrow his eyebrows, frown, and hasten his steps in the opposite direction. Now, I'm not an overly sensitive person, but after about four of those non encounters, I was beginning to feel like a rejected mail order bride.

Exhausted and discouraged, I collapsed onto a bench to devise a new plan. My eyes downcast in thought, I noticed with a horrified gasp that my ankles were enormous, the size of elephant ankles! Oh, those blasted pantyhose! Thirty hours of having my circulation cinched off at the waist had surely caused this humiliating monstrosity. I bent over, undoubtedly in a most unladylike fashion, to try to massage my ankles back down to a normal size. Then I reminded myself that this was no time for vanity and that I must take such thoughts captive and focus on... "Why, of course!" I thought as the light went on, "This must be a TEST!"

My boss was probably hiding somewhere in that arrival hall, watching to see how I'd handle a crisis like not being picked up upon arrival in a foreign country where I couldn't speak the language. Would I rise to the occasion or crumble in the face of a challenge? Remembering that I had been given emergency numbers to call in just such a situation, I dug through my carefully organized travel documents and triumphantly pulled out the numbers. The next trick was to find a phone. Fortunately, phones look the same everywhere, so it was easy to communicate my need using simple body language. A porter directed me to the phones on the wall and led me right there himself, in fact. Oh, I was going to like it here, I decided, with such kind, helpful people everywhere.

There I stood at the phone, ready to use my numbers, when it occurred to me that the phone here probably wasn't going to take my quarters, the ones my father always told me never to leave home without.

My blank stare must have given away my predicament to the porter, who graciously reached into his pocket and put his own coins into the phone for me. The first number I called gave me a piercing tone followed by a bilingual message telling me the number I had dialed was no longer in service. The second number I dialed rang and rang with no answer. "Wow," I thought to myself, a little mystified, "this is some initiation. I wonder what I have to do to pass? But no one's worried here!" I coached myself, using my usual state the opposite mantra, "No one feels like crying right now... " I finally decided to just sit there on a bench, too tired to wander back around the arrival hall for the umpteenth time, accosting more foreigners.

Within thirty seconds, a petite Indonesian man approached me carrying a tiny piece of crinkled white paper, perhaps only five inches long and one inch high, with my name written on it. I don't know when I've ever been so happy to see my name! Filled with relief, I could have hugged that little man except that I was afraid that a.) I might snap his back, or b.) I might have to marry him. This Prince Charming led me not to my boss, but to my boss's wife. His petite, olive skinned, brown eyed, jet black haired wife!

Lessons for the traveler:

1. Ixnay on anty hosepay for long journeys.

2. No need to panic or fear if things don't as expected, especially as you first arrive. Try to be resourceful as you need to be, and in a pinch, just sit and wait.

3. Do not assume you know about someone purely based on his or her appearance.

2

The Trumpet Sounding

Despite the complications of finding my ride home in the busy Jakarta airport, I was excited to see all the new sights and scenes in the bustling city of 10 million people from all over the world. Nevertheless, I was exhausted, ankles still swollen, and it was HOT there, even hotter and more humid than steamy Charleston, South Carolina which I'd left a mere thirty two hours ago. Charleston could be scorching in June, but Jakarta seemed more smothering, perhaps because of all the congested highways and the miles and miles of 80 plus story skyscrapers. My boss lived in a typical neighbor-hood, tucked in behind curvy, narrow streets lined with open sewers.

Knowing I was in a dilapidated state after such a long journey, my gracious hosts welcomed me, fed me dinner, showed me the shower, and let me go right to bed. I don't remember what I dreamt, or if I even stirred, but I do recall exactly how I awoke. It was sudden. It was LOUD. It was still dark outside, when I heard… what? What in the world was that sound?! Was it sirens? What WAS it? Extreme fatigue, coupled with the dreamlike experience of being in a place so mysterious and different from what I was used to conspired to make me quick to jump to spiritual conclusions in my exhausted brain as I pondered the ongroing noise. Was it…? Could it be…? "Oh, have mercy! I know it's not, but.. what IF, what if... it's the trumpet sounding?!" I marveled, my heart racing. You know, THE trumpet sounding, the one that signifies the long awaited return of Christ; as in 'the trumpet shall sound and the dead shall be raised,' trumpet?!" I felt kind of disappointed because my hair was all mussed up and I still had morning dragon breath, but, oh well, when it's time, it's time. So I just sat up in bed, arranged my hair hurriedly with my fingers as best I could, rubbed my eyes and face one time to remove anything unsightly and tilted my face upward with a peaceful smile, ready to ascend, just in case. "Okay, Lord," I thought, "I'm as ready as I can be with no notice."

But obviously I did not ascend. I remained still, in that position, face lifted to the heavens, for as long as the sound continued. The sound faded away, and there was silence. There I sat, mystified. "Was that it? Surely I didn't miss it. I mean, I KNOW I was ready," I reasoned, but I could feel a panic of the unknown building within my pounding heart, nonetheless. I scrambled to the bedroom door and flung it open to see if anyone in the house was unfortunate enough to be left behind, too. But it was still dark outside, early morning, so not a creature was stirring, not even a gecko.

There was nothing to do but wait and pray, mostly wait, I confess. After what seemed an eternity, I heard movement, and peeked out the door to see the helper rustling around in the kitchen. That was a good start, but didn't really confirm anything because I didn't know where she stood on such matters and I didn't have the language to ask her. I wanted to see my boss or his wife because, if nothing else, misery loves company and the tribulation years weren't going to be too fun.

Finally, I heard my boss's bedroom door creek open and, YES, it was his wife! What a beautiful sight! She didn't seem the least bit upset, which indicated that her husband was still there beside her when she woke up. She noticed me standing there and greeted me with a big smile,

"Good morning! Did you sleep well?"

"Oh, yes, I slept just fine, thank you," I nodded, which was technically the truth. "Umm, did you hear something this morning?" I queried.

"Hear something? Like what? Were the neighborhood kids too noisy? They sometimes go out and play a bit before going to school," she answered matter of factly.

"Well, no, this wasn't children. It was a real blaring sound, but muffled so that I couldn't pick up exactly what it was. In my pre awake, jet lagged stupor, I actually thought it was the trumpet sounding," I half kidded.

"THE trumpet?" She turned to face me, with a quizzical look. "Oh no. That was the call to prayer from the mosque across the street behind the house. Have you never heard it before? It goes off five times a day; we hardly notice it anymore. Welcome to Indonesia!"

Ah… the call to prayer… how familiar it would soon become. Yes, welcome to Indonesia.

Lessons for the Traveler:

1. Jet lag is real. Try not to draw conclusions or make decisions while still in jet lag.

2. Might be advisable to familiarize oneself with the call to prayer before entering a Muslim country; it is available on the internet.

3

Divine Appointments
and Spoken Blessings

As much as I appreciated my boss's hospitality in Jakarta, I could hardly contain my eagerness to see *my* province. I was eager to be introduced to the person I'd live with for two years, Lisa, and to look into the faces of my new neighbors, students, and friends. The flight in was uneventful except for the fact that I sat beside a lovely Indonesian woman, probably in her 60's, who could speak English quite well. There on the plane, she taught me the polite way to greet people in her area and pronounced, prophetically,

"I think you'll find your time here like *Alice in Wonderland.*"

In spite of my natural anxiety, I looked into her eyes, so warm and welcoming, so excited on my behalf, so sure her countrymen would be kind to me, and affirmed,

"Yes, I feel quite sure it will. Thank you."

I never saw her again, but I have thought of that sweet woman so many times, thankful that she was the one to usher me into my new life. It wasn't the first time a stranger had spoken a blessing over me, though.

When I was eighteen years old and a freshman at the University of North Carolina,Chapel Hill, I flew home to California for Fall break. From Raleigh Durham to Dallas, there was a man on my row, with an empty seat between us. He was quite a friendly fellow, but not creepily so. I was taken aback by this man's story at first, because I couldn't imagine why he felt the need to impress me, just a kid in a sweatshirt. He had been at a lawyers' convention, he told me, as the keynote speaker. With a gleam of mischief in his eye he confided,

"But I didn't tell them what they thought I would. You see, I'm the most famous defense attorney in the world. Really, you may check the *Guinness Book of World Records* and find my name there officially as the most successful defense attorney—never lost a case."

Seeing my surprise, he handed me a business card with his name, along with his business address in Dallas. 'Sir Lionel A. Luckhoo,' it read. He then went on to describe his illustrious career and his great prestige as a politician and diplomat. He told me that he knew what it was like to be rich and powerful, but that something had happened to make him realize that it was all worth nothing in comparison.

By then I was leaning forward, eager to hear what it was that had so utterly transformed his perspective. He gave his testimony of coming to faith in Jesus Christ, and turning his life over to this newfound Savior. He said his wife had left him in frustration over his new priorities, but he'd never looked back. He went on to relate that he was often invited to lawyers' conventions because of his status, but that he always presented the Gospel when he got there.

By that time I really WAS impressed! This man was so bold and had chosen his faith above everything the world values. I can't recall if Mr. Luckhoo said anything particularly specific for me because my mind was so wrapped up in his amazing testimony. But I distinctly remember that when lunch was served, he asked if he could say grace for us, and he extended his hand to hold mine while he prayed. He said a prayer for me, and I was moved by what a kind and generous person he seemed to be, especially for someone so famous.

Sir Lionel A. Luckhoo and I parted in Dallas and I never saw him again, but I was left with an extraordinary sense of blessing that day. When I arrived in San Francisco, I immediately reported this divine appointment to my parents, who guffawed and told me how ridiculous that was. They insisted that whoever that man was, he certainly was *not* anyone famous; and they surely hoped a fine education at UNC would teach me not to be so gullible. I insisted that before even leaving the airport we stop at a bookstore and just take a peek in the Guinness Book of World Records to see if he was in there or not. I was, after all, still clutching his business card, so he was not a figment of my imagination. Besides, his story was too outrageous not to be true. So, glad to have a teachable moment, my parents indulged me and LO and BEHOLD, there he was, Sir Lionel A Luckhoo!

Incidents like these, Mr. Luckhoo from October of 1983 and the unnamed Indonesian woman fourteen years later, convinced me that speaking blessings over others is worth taking seriously. It's a privilege and honor to be on either end of such an exchange.

Lessons for the Traveler:

1. People are put into our lives to teach us and bless us. Receive the blessing.

2. We are put into others' lives to teach them and bless them. Be the blessing.

4

Shopping In Bali

I've never been a big shopper. Somehow I just missed that gene, and have likened looking through racks of clothes to having bamboo shoots shoved up my fingernails. Even as a kid, I was perfectly happy if Mom just ordered clothes from the Sears and Roebuck Catalog, which accounts for the poor fashion sense that plagues me to this day. In Bali, however, I learned a new way to shop that pales in torture quotient to plodding through malls. In Bali, the sales people come to the shopper, right there on the beach. Yes, there are plenty of formal markets and stores to delight true shoppers. But the beach areas are fair territory for vendors.

The beaches on Bali are famous world wide for their stellar beauty, with the sprawling white sand and the clear blue green water, a truly exotic environment. My roommate Lisa hadn't been there either, so at our first opportunity, we put on shorts and went for a walk along the beach. At first, the sellers seemed innocuous enough, calling out to see if we wanted to buy their wares. Lisa answered tersely and kept walking because others had told her this was the only way to avoid a calamitous swarming effect.

I, on the other hand, saw no harm in exercising my Southern manners and made eye contact with each person who spoke to me, answering,

"No, thank you," with a smile.

Having been brought up by Betty Crocker (my mother, not the cook), I was no ugly American. Within ten minutes, there was a horde of beach vendors surrounding me, asking again and again if I'd like to buy their bracelets, have my hair braided, etc. It sounded something like this:

Beach vendor #1: Hello Miss. You wanna buy a bracelet? *Alice*: No, thank you.

Beach vendor #1: Come on, I give you good price. Low price. How many you want? *Alice*: No, no, really, I don't want any. Thank you anyway.

Beach vendor #1: I have many colors. Here, you try this one (The saleslady takes my arm and puts it on me. I start to object, but I'm distracted by a second beach vendor).

Beach vendor #2: Okay I braid your hair. You look real pretty. *Alice*: Oh no, no. I don't want my hair braided... no, thank you.

Beach vendor #2: No problem. Cheap. I give you cheap. You look pretty after. (The second beach vendor grabs part of my hair, pulling me down, causing me to bend over at an awkward angle because I'm so tall.) *Alice*: Hey, wait a minute!

Stop that! I don't want my hair braided! (Then, to beach vendor #1, who was busy adding bracelets to the wrist she held in bondage,) And I'm not buying a bracelet, either!

Beach vendor #3: You need shorts. I got pretty shorts. They look good on you. Big size! *Alice*: Oh, no thank you. I don't need shorts… Hey, let go of my leg!

Finally, Lisa came bursting through the crowd to drag me out of the chaos, peeling the ladies' hands and goods off of me and guiding me to safety, where I stood bewildered.

"How did that happen? I was saying 'No' the whole time!" I wailed, confused.

"I don't know. All I know is that I was talking to you and glanced over to see you missing and only one of your flip flops left!" Lisa explained, laughing. "Oh," she continued, wagging her head, "I wish I had my camera."

Lessons to the Traveler:

1. Southern manners do not apply on the beaches of Bali.

2. The sellers don't intend you any harm; they're just trying to make a living, so no need for offense or anger. Just keep walking if you're not interested in buying anything.

3. Best to travel in pairs. Isn't there a verse in Proverbs about that?

5

Almost Drowning

It's interesting how a near death experience can become a landmark in a person's journey that serves as a source of encouragement for the rest of his or her life. I have had several near car accidents that could have been ugly had they occurred, but there was only one time when I really thought I was going to die.

It happened at a beautiful beach on the western tip of my beloved province in Indonesia. I hadn't been in the country long, maybe three months or so, when our supervisor summoned all the English teachers on our team from throughout the province to his house for a meeting. After one morning of intense training, we took the afternoon off to hang out at the beach. I was floating on my back, just relaxing in the water, daydreaming, when I decided I should go in to re apply my sunscreen. When I looked up, I realized I had floated out way beyond where I'd intended. I didn't panic, though, because I was a decent swimmer. I just put my head down and swam freestyle until I felt winded. I figured I was probably about halfway in.

In fact, the current had carried me even further out! I began to feel nervous, but I reminded myself that both my supervisor and his wife had been lifeguards, so, though embarrassing, if push came to shove, I could holler out for one of them to come help me. First, however, I wanted to try my best to get to shore on my own.

So, I put my head back down and swam with more intensity, pulling hard with my arms and kicking with my legs. I needed to make some forward progress. Again, I swam and swam until I felt tired, but I didn't want to swim to the point of exhaustion. When I looked up, I saw that I'd only moved forward a few yards. I reminded myself not to panic, and I steeled myself to endure the humiliation of having to be saved. I knew I was in trouble. With every ounce of energy I could muster, I called for help to my supervisor's wife on the shore.

"GWEEEEEENNN!" I yelled.

But Gwen couldn't hear me. I was too far out. Panic set in. There was going to be no help that day except from the Lord Himself if, indeed, I still had time on this earth. I put my head down and drove my arms into the water again and again, kicking ferociously. I thought, "I'll get back to that coast or die trying." It occurred to me that my life might end that very day. I prayed, "Lord, I was a fool to let myself drift out so far, and it may be that this is as far as You intended for me to travel on this earth; but I haven't done anything for You yet. If I die today in this water, everyone back home will call me a brave hero for going across the world to help people, but in fact, I'm just a fool. If there's any way, Lord, please help me. Please help me get back to shore."

When I couldn't push any further, I stopped long enough to see where I was. I could barely reach my toes to the sand below, which filled me with relief and hope; but a wave came and picked me up again so I could no longer reach the bottom. With a second wind, I thrust myself forward again, putting my head down and doggedly pulling with my arms and kicking with my legs.

"We're almost there, Lord. Just a little further. If I don't have to die today, I'll be SO thankful!"

Again, near the point of exhaustion, I looked up, and set my feet down solidly on the sand below. The water was only up to my thighs. I was going to make it after all! I could no longer think or pray. It took all my remaining strength just to put one foot in front of the other, because I still had to fight the vicious undertow. Oddly, it was when the water was only up to my knees that I distinctly heard the words,

"Just lay down and die in the water. You'll never make it."

And I almost did just that. I stumbled onto my knees before reality hit,

"Wait, I'm not in danger anymore. I'm safe. The Lord delivered me. I don't have to die today. I'm alright! Why would I give up NOW?!"

With that final burst of energy, I plodded completely out of the water and fell onto the sand, dead tired. A co worker walked by and asked if I was okay.

"I am now!" was all I could say.

It was strange how it hadn't occurred to me to quit trying until I was already *out* of danger. How clear that voice was, although it was obviously not from the One who loves me, and, in my utter exhaustion, how tempted I was to obey.

I've often thought about that day, particularly when discouraged or feeling useless. The Lord frequently reminds me that if He didn't have a plan for my future, He could have let me drown that Saturday afternoon, carried off to the middle of the ocean. He reminds me that the voice that told me to just lie down and die wasn't His... And I am comforted, my strength and hope renewed.

We call such experiences *Ebenezer moments*, times when God shows Himself mightily to save against all odds, overcoming even our own stark stupidity or carelessness. I'm grateful to have such markers in my life, but I will be glad when they are no longer necessary.

Lessons to the Traveler:

1. God is big enough to overcome our foolishness, but best to seek and exercise wisdom from Him as we go.

2. Any voice of self destruction is NOT from the Lord.

3. Pay attention whenever in the water; the undertow can be deceptively dangerous.

6

The Wedding Shuffle

I'll never forget the day I made my debut in local social life by attending my neighbor's wedding. I had been in the country only two months, still in the honeymoon stage of transition, so I was excited to absorb every morsel of cultural experience possible. The party was held at the bride's home, directly across the street from our house. Weddings in Indonesia are marvelous social events. Special landscaping is done around the host's house to accommodate and impress the throng of relatives, friends, business associates, and neighbors attending the party. Depending on the wealth and popularity of the host, there can be up to 2000 guests invited.

A typical wedding party has at least 300 to 500 guests, who wear their formal attire to participate in the celebration. All of the main rooms of the house are decorated to the hilt, covering the walls, even the ceiling, with gorgeous brightly colored, ornate material so as to transform the home into a virtual palace for the grand occasion. The bride and groom don elaborate wedding costumes, and they sit on a specially designed platform, where guests file by for hours on end to wish them well and offer gifts. Being Caucasian always warranted special treatment for my roommate Lisa and me because we were obviously "not from around these parts."

On this auspicious occasion, as always, cameras were flashing all around us and other guests were prodding us to sing with the keyboard blaring on the platform in the front yard. When it was time to bestow blessings upon the couple, the host encouraged us to come inside and see the ceremony. I was delighted. Everyone takes pictures throughout the festivities, so I would have no problem scoring some great shots.

When we entered the house, we saw Ibus (pronounced eebooz, i.e. ladies older than ourselves) sitting side by side on the floor, lining the walls around the room. Lisa sat her little rear end down right beside the front door, leaving me to find my own significantly larger space in which to put my own derriere. Before I could do much looking, the Ibu I presume was the wedding coordinator took my hand and led me around the house to let me take pictures. Since I had to pass the Ibus lining the walls, I assumed the polite position when passing in front of seated people: stooping over, lowering my head, and hanging my right arm straight down, folding my left arm neatly behind my back. Not a particularly attractive nor graceful position for a 5'9 heavy set girl, but it showed the appropriate respect for the women I was passing, and that was the point.

After I had snapped a few shots, the coordinator enthusiastically shook my hand and thanked me, which I thought was my cue to be dismissed. So I made my way back past all the Ibus to the front door where Lisa had settled. She asked me where I was going and I informed her that I thought something private was supposed to happen, because the lady had dismissed me. Lisa assured me that I must stay to see the ceremony. I insisted that I must step outside, but said I would leave my camera with Lisa to take pictures of the highlights. As I started to give her my camera, the coordinator saw me, and made a bee line over to us to be sure I did not leave.

"Please," she gestured and told me in Indonesian, "sit down."

So I re entered the room, smiling and stooping to show respect again, and a classic *Alice moment* began. All of the Ibus' eyes were glued to me as I tried to find a space to sit that was large enough to accommodate my comparatively voluminous fanny. Maintaining my slightly stooped position, I took a couple of steps one direction, heeding the assistance of some kind Ibus who were suggesting,

"Over here... here…here…"

After scooting over to the recommended space and seeing that said space was clearly not large enough, I would take a few steps back in retreat, then head in another direction, following the voices of other Ibus calling and gesturing to other possible spots where I might fit. Smiling and querying softly,

"Di mana?" (Where?), I continued in that ridiculous fashion, doing something of a shuffle amidst the growing chaos of everyone trying to help me.

The Ibus felt sorry for me, poor, bungling, white giant, but they could hardly hide their amusement and took little effort to muffle their giggles at my plight. I looked with desperation to the bride and mouthed,

"Ma'af!" (Sorry) because I surely had no intention of stealing the attention that should have been exclusively theirs on this day.

She and her groom smiled graciously and nodded with compassion. One elderly woman in particular was so tickled, I was afraid she soon might need medical attention. Eventually, much to my relief, I found a seat in a back corner, away from the front room. The wrinkly Ibu in hysterics leaned around to continue laughing "with" me and, for a moment, I thought she was actually going to give me a high five.

The whole *Alice wedding shuffle* probably lasted all of twenty seconds, but to me, it seemed an eternity. One might wonder what was Lisa doing in the midst of this crisis? As I recall, I heard her voice among the Ibus', saying

"Over there…no, over there…oh no, not there…" and contributing to the melee.

Tears had welled up in her eyes from laughing so hard at my awkward situation. Admittedly, she was no help whatsoever.

"I just couldn't think of anything to do!" she said in defense, "I was laughing too hard! Oh, I wish I had my camera."

With friends like these...

Lessons for the Traveler:

1. Humorous situations create strong bonds between people, even strangers, so no need to overreact to awkward moments.

Smile and keep moving.

2. Genuine efforts to fit into a new culture with respect are generally met with kindness and mercy.

3. If you're laughing too, others are laughing with you, not at you. Keep telling yourself that.

7

Choosing a Language Tutor

When Lisa and I first moved into our neighborhood, we struggled with how two single American women could live in a Muslim community without people expecting us to open a brothel. A friend from the Education Department recommended that we find an adopted father figure, a respected Muslim man who would be viewed as responsible for us and who could vouch for our character. We didn't have to look far to find a suitable candidate for the role. Our next door neighbors had in their employ a Javanese man in his late fifties named Pak Tarkim.

The father of twelve, Pak Tarkim was a diligent worker and capable gardener, so he came to work for, and watch over, Lisa and me. As part of his program to see that we adapted well to our new culture, Pak Tarkim constantly introduced new vocabulary to us. He also peppered us with questions about English words, so our house was an informal language learning environment for all three of us. Lisa and I soon realized that it was entirely possible that Pak Tarkim would learn English faster than we would learn Indonesian.

Two months after renting our house, our boss gave us permission to have a *western potty* put into the bigger bathroom. The owner agreed to put in clean new tile and a sink, too, the works! This renovation took several days, so I hung around the house in case the workers needed anything Pak Tarkim couldn't get for them. I had had several brief conversations with the lead worker when he asked me if I had a certain item. I didn't recognize the word, so he described what it was.

"Ah, of course! That's a _____ ," I said, using the vocabulary word for that item that Pak Tarkim had taught me. "Yes, let me get it."

I was sure the young man would be impressed that I had such a handle on his country's vocabulary since I knew the correct word for an item when, evidently, he only knew the slang term for it. In the kitchen, I secured the desired item and presented it to him with a satisfied look on my face.

"Here's your tool, _____."

I was sure to pronounce the word slowly and carefully so he could remember to ask for it *properly* on future job sites. The young man hesitated a moment, then said,

"You know ma'am. It's really called a _____," he explained, the way he had said it the first time.

"No," I rebutted cheerfully, "He (and I gestured to Pak Tarkim, who was busily weeding the garden across the yard) told me it was _____," and I repeated my masterly vocabulary.

"Ma'am," the worker said with a pained look on his face, sorry to burst my bubble, "He only says it that way because he's missing his front teeth!"

Lessons for the Traveler:

1. Best to imitate the language of tutors who have a full set of teeth and no language impediments.

2. Learning, or at least checking, vocabulary from several sources is advisable.

8

Pak Tarkim's Remarkable Spatial Skills

Indonesians have remarkable spatial skills. They can accurately guess the measurements of a room at a mere glance, or fearlessly whoosh by another vehicle within inches because they KNOW they're not going to hit it. I think it comes from living in close quarters, but I can't really explain it. A perfect example was our gardener and protector, Pak Tarkim. Not long after I had come to town, Pak Tarkim could no longer contain his astonishment and curiosity and had to know just how much would such an enormous person weigh?! So, one afternoon as I was leaving the house, he asked me directly,

"Just how much DO you weigh?! About # kilograms?"

Shocked, horrified, incensed, but without any idea of what that figure meant in pounds, I expressed how offended I was that he would guess such a high number, and stomped back into the house to find my calculator. Feverishly punching in the numbers to find out how many kilograms I *really* weighed, I was dashed to see that he had guessed correctly, to the ounce. Embarrassed, but impressed, I was set free that day from the illusion that there would be anything private in my life during my time in Indonesia. I realized that the average person could, with one look, assess my weight in terms of equivalent sacks of rice.

Lessons for the Traveler:

1. Try not to be overly offended by comments about your body. There's no offense intended, and it is usually just making an observation.

2. No need to cling to the fantasy that your personal information is private. Your neighbors know. They do.

3. Learn the metric system as soon as possible. It will be helpful on a daily basis.

9

Along Came Ita

Growing up a military brat, I moved every three years. This transient lifestyle necessitated a strategy for making friends in a new place quickly. We always moved in June, after school let out for the summer. My goal was to have kids to sit with at the lunch table at school by September, so I had no time to waste. The most effective method I found was to get involved in team sports. When we moved to a new place, Betty Crocker would immediately sign me up for summer league playing anything: soccer, basketball, softball, whatever was available, so I could make friends before the school year began. It never failed.

When I moved overseas, I employed the same strategy. How well loved I felt by the Lord when I saw there was a volleyball court in the field diagonally across the street from our house. Every afternoon, after the 4:00 prayer time, ladies from the neighborhood would gather on that court, remove cow droppings with a shovel, and play spirited volleyball. For average housewives, the level of play was quite high, using the bump, set, hit model. And some of those ladies, though only 5'2 to perhaps 5'6 in height, had ferocious spikes and serves.

Every afternoon, I would go to the edge of our fenced in yard and just watch, lacking the courage to invite myself into the game because I couldn't speak the language.

One day, the ladies had already started playing when one of the players ran by our house, late to practice. She saw me standing there, and stopped dead in her tracks. This beautiful woman, about 5'2" with straight black hair cut in a cute bob around her round face, looked right at me, extended her right arm my direction, and waved her fingers pointing down, towards me.

"Who? Me?" I gestured, looking behind me. I knew it HAD to be me, but I was so excited, I couldn't believe it.

"Yes," she nodded, "You!" and she waved her arm with a larger motion, making sure I knew it was an invitation to go with her.

Elated, I squealed and dashed into the house to grab my sneakers.

"Lisa! Let's play volleyball!" I hollered, as I ran by her room. So we put on our gear and joined the ladies. I hadn't played in a long time so my skills weren't stellar, and I couldn't say anything, but we had a wonderful time. We played and laughed, and used expressions and hand signals that were clear enough to communicate rudimentary ideas. I left that dirt court on cloud nine; the ladies could not have been friendlier to Lisa and me.

The next day, I studied the phrase, "I'm glad to see you again," in my language book, practicing until I felt confident I could use it to greet my new friend. The clock finally struck 4:30 and I ran out to play with the ladies, who greeted me with big smiles. But the lady who had invited me the day before wasn't there. I was disappointed because I wanted to try out my new phrase on her. I don't know why I didn't try it out on the other ladies, but I didn't. The lady with the bob somehow seemed more open to me because she had taken the initiative to communicate with me, a stranger from a foreign land.

The following afternoon, I was thrilled to see my friend with the bob out there. She smiled broadly when I approached, flashing those spectacular pearly whites of hers. I nodded a greeting to everyone, but walked right up to her.

"I'm glad to see you again."

There was an awkward silence, filled only by another player asking,

"What did she say?"

This gracious woman with the bob looked at the others and stated proudly,

"She said, 'I'm glad to see you again,' " in the exact words and intonation I had used.

The other ladies laughed with glee partly because they were pleasantly surprised to hear me speak their language, and partly because, I later learned, that the way I had phrased that greeting was very formal and stiff. The lovely lady in the bob then turned back to me and said, using my unnatural words and intonation,

"I'm glad to see you again, too."

My heart could have exploded with joy! I had found a friend! This nice woman had been willing to suffer the teasing of others to repeat my greeting precisely in that clumsy fashion back to me, to be sure I would understand her. I had successfully communicated the message and this woman had responded sweetly. It was a glorious first step.She then continued her kindness.

"Ita. My name is Ita," she said, very slowly, gesturing to herself.

I then told everyone my name, which was difficult for them to pronounce because of the flat "A" sound at the beginning. But they tried and I tried to say their names, too. I was so thankful Ita's name was easy to say and remember, for she had already staked a claim in my heart. Thus a beautiful friendship began.

To this day, Ita is one of my closest friends and we talk regularly. My wonderful experience in Indonesia was largely due to Ita's taking me under her wing from that first invitation to play volleyball. At Ita's house, I learned about everything Indonesian: language, culture, food, etiquette, Indonesian music, and Islamic practices. I could ask her anything and she would take me with her wherever she went, correcting me when I needed correcting and helping me when I needed help. I could tell a thousand stories about Ita and her four beautiful children, her delightful mother, amiable siblings, and other relatives that filled my eleven years in Indonesia with joy. With Ita, I scored an Indonesian family of my own.

As I had left the United States, I had prayed a simple prayer, asking God to give me just one true friend who would be honest with me. And the friends and joy He showered over me through those years cannot be numbered or recounted in full. But at the foundation of every other blessing laid the extreme kindness and generosity of this one woman, three years my junior, mother of four, who took the risk to extend a hand to a person the world would tell her should have been her enemy. Having started with Ita as my first friend, I was naturally predisposed to expect the very best from Indonesians everywhere I went. American and Indonesian friends alike have heard numerous Ita stories, and have marveled with me that God was so good to me to bring such a faithful friend into my path. I'll be forever thankful for Ita, and I wouldn't be surprised if readers of these stories come to love her, too.

Lessons for the Traveler:

1. Never underestimate the value of a close friend from the host country. He or she can smooth the paths into society and surround you with a ring of care and protection.

2. Get involved in neighborhood activities as soon as possible to demonstrate camaraderie. The more active the event, the less language you'll need.

3. Remember that there is risk for the host country person to reach out to a foreigner, so appreciate the heart of anyone who extends a hand to you.

10

Being an Umbrella

By the end of the fourth month in my new land, I felt that I was being better accepted, largely because my behind was being handled more readily by my new friends. Often I wasn't sure if it was affection or morbid curiosity. It was perfectly acceptable in that area for friends of the same gender to walk down the road arm in arm, with interlocked fingers, arms around hips, etc. As flattered as I was to be well liked, I confess this was not one of my easier paradigm shifts, given my propensity to be easily embarrassed. For one thing, I was so much taller than my friends that when being affectionate and putting their arms around me, the height of their arms often meant that their hands were very near, if not covering my… well, the general area that plumbers often reveal when bending over. I always knew it was obvious where a friend's hand was when I would hear Lisa cackle,

"Oh, I wish I had my camera."

One Saturday, we left for a volleyball tournament at seven in the morning. Fortunately, the event was in town, so we could take pedicabs with our friends to the court. We had a good team, but we were worn out by the end of the second match. Plus, it was very hot. The jet black hair on my friends' heads absorbed the sun's rays, so they struggled with the heat even more than I did.

Between matches, as we stood along the sidelines watching other teams play, one friend commented that she was extremely hot. One by one, ladies began to crowd around me, to my left and in front of me. I thought to myself,

"Wow, these ladies really like me. It must be the love of God that is a magnet to them, drawing them closer and closer."

This illusion was immediately dashed, however, when one overheated friend peered up at me and said one of the few words she knew in English,

"Umbrella."

Ah, yes, umbrella… my friends had realized that if they stood close enough to me they could find shade. Very nice. So, there I stood, sandwiched between teammates in the sweltering heat, feeling appreciated, cared for, needed, and ready to fall over. As they became tired, the ladies felt free to lean on me, too. One woman who felt sorry for me tossed a white hand towel on my head to keep the sun off of me. Such a thoughtful gesture, really. I looked over at Lisa, a human resting post with a towel on my head and she laughed, as always, regretting she didn't have her camera.

During the tournament, I noticed that my name had become "Helless" because the flat "A" sound in Alice is difficult for Indonesians to pronounce. Also, I could tell that the commentator mentioned me in almost every sentence during our games because I heard the words "Australian," and "buleh" (foreigner) echoing through the enormous speakers around the court. I'm American, but my teammates didn't correct him, so I pretended not to understand anything, which wasn't far from the truth. When I would call for the ball or cheer for my team, I would immediately hear the voice of the announcer's, along with many others' rendition of what I had just said. By the end of the day, I had grown weary of that.

Sometimes, people would just come up, squat right in front of where I was sitting, and stare at me, smiling. They wouldn't try to speak to me in any language, nor bother me, but just stare. My friend told me it was because they were mesmerized to see my blue eyes. I heard my new name at least a thousand times that day. I sometimes wondered what was being said, but decided it was best to just appreciate feeling accepted.

Lessons for the Traveler:

1. People might well openly stare at you because you look different, particularly in outlying areas where there are not many foreigners. No need to be offended. Just smile, speak a greeting, and carry on with whatever you were doing.

2. Try not to shrink back from the looser same gender physical boundaries, realizing its innocence; but do not, repeat, do not, try this upon returning to the U.S.

3. When you hear a reference to yourself, then laughter, do not assume the person is mocking you. It's not personal, just entertainment. Pretend you don't hear it, or smile along.

11

Exposed Pillowcases

One day, I was minding my own business in my house, when Ita and her youngest sister Didit came bolting through the front door and whizzed by me to the side porch where my undergarments were drying on the clothes line. I followed them out there, wondering what could cause such a stir. Ita was feverishly snatching my undies off the line and re hanging them such that they were folded down the middle, with one leg hole on either side of the line, rather than splayed out in their full glory as I'd hung them. In America, we'd never folded clothes over the line. We'd hung them up so the sun could dry the whole garment at once. Seeing my confusion, Didit, in her early twenties, shook a pair of my undies in my direction and said with vexation,

"What are these, pillowcases?! Get them off the line!"

Ita, being more of a people pleaser than her sister, and more familiar with my naivety, explained,

"Bi, we don't hang our private garments out like that so everyone can see the crotch. It's very rude."

"Oh, dear, I'm very sorry. But here on the side porch, do you think anyone will see them?"

"See them?!" interjected Ita's sister, "How could we NOT see them: jumbo and white, casting a glare onto the street like a billboard?! It would be bad enough if they were little panties, but these... !" she held them up for emphasis.

Somehow they did seem gargantuan, downright unsightly, in the hands of this petite beauty.

"Oh no," she continued, "these don't even need to be outside to dry. You need a rack for inside. Just set them near a window."

I glanced over at Ita, who was nodding in agreement, though not with her sister's fervor. I thanked them for informing me of such important cultural information and assured them that the sun would not set that day before I had a drying rack on which to hang my "pillowcases." Satisfied by having saved their foreign friend from yet another flagrant indiscretion, Ita and Didit went home wondering what I would ever do without them.

Lessons for the Traveler:

1. Adult undergarments are not for public display, period.

2. When caught committing a cultural faux pas, no need to justify or explain it, just apologize and rectify the situation.

3. Appreciate honest friends. They will help you as much as you'll let them.

12

Language Bloopers
and Frightening a Local Celebrity

One of the dangers of language learning is mixing up words that sound similar; sound similar to the learner, that is, thus opening the door for the dreaded spoonerism. Spoonerisms are words or phrases in which letters or syllables get turned around, or swapped. In English, an example of this would be to say "tips of the slung" instead of "slip of the tongue." Here, there were some words that acted like spoonerisms even though the pronunciation of either word is correct, just having another meaning. For example, learners of Indonesian sometimes mistake the word, "kepala," meaning 'head' for the word "kelapa," meaning coconut. That, however, is not my story. No, I laughed about others making such silly mistakes until the day I added my own contribution to the language blooper list.

Like every area throughout Indonesian society, our neighborhood had a "leader of the street," who was the one responsible for handling administrative matters or problems within his designated zone of about 100 households. Our street leader lived just down the road, in fact. His wife was very beautiful, and highly respected as a devout Muslim, skilled in teaching other women to read their holy book with precision in pitch and pronunciation. She was lovely, the type of woman who turned heads with her modest style. She didn't plod along like the rest of us, but rather seemed to glide effortlessly, gracefully. Never was a drop of sweat to be found on her brow nor a socially acceptable burp released from her lips. Lisa and I would stop what we were doing when she passed by our house just to get a glimpse of her. How royal she seemed, looking our way, nodding with such a benevolent smile. "She's so elegant," we would whisper.

When I mentioned to my friend Ita the star like effect the street leader's wife had on us, Ita agreed.

"Oh, it's not just you two; we feel the same way about her. Isn't she stunning? We often discuss how sometimes she takes our breath away," Ita confessed, "and a bunch of us ladies in the neighborhood gather at her house every Friday afternoon to learn how to better recite the verses of our holy book. She knows all the meanings and has a wonderful voice."

I asked Ita what her name was, and she said that she didn't know.

"We just call her 'the street leader's wife.'"

I suppose that was because it would have been disrespectful to just call her by name like common folk. Ita's confirmation that there was something special about the street leader's wife made me feel better, because it was strange to nearly swoon at the sight of a neighbor, a woman nonetheless.

How delighted I was, then, when one afternoon as I was

on my way home from town on my motorcycle, I noticed the street leader's wife walking along the side of the road. She was heading in the direction of her house, but was still a good half mile away, so I thought how great it would be to give her a lift, then brag to Lisa when I got home. I felt a little nervous as I greeted our neighborhood celebrity,

"Good afternoon, Ma'am!" I said, removing my helmet.

"Good afternoon!" she answered in her gentle voice, flashing that gorgeous smile of hers.

"Um, would you like a ride home on my motorcycle? I'd be happy to take you," I offered in my best, most polite Indonesian.

"No, thank you. That won't be necessary," she answered, still smiling.

It occurred to me that she might be afraid because I was relatively new in town and hadn't been riding a motorcycle long, so I tried to reassure her,

"Are you sure? I know how to 'bencong!' " [an Indonesian word I thought meant to tote someone on the back of one's motorcycle].

The street leader's wife's smile disappeared, replaced by a look of confusion, perhaps dismay.

"Oh no, I'm quite sure. Thank you, anyway!" she said, smiling again, though a bit nervously, it seemed.

"Well, okay then," I acquiesced, "Have a nice afternoon, Ma'am."

I rode off, dashed, thinking dejectedly that she must not like foreigners. "Maybe she didn't want to ride with me because she thinks I only pray on Sundays." I ruminated. As always when I had something happen that brought me joy or sadness, victory or defeat, I went directly to my friend Ita's to recount my experience.

"Ita!" I called, hesitating briefly as I entered her house. Like most houses that didn't have air conditioning, the doors at Ita's house stayed wide open when there was someone home.

"Yeah, Bi, back here!" Ita called from the washing area in the rear of the house. I joined Ita in the back.

"Where are you coming from?" she inquird in the common Indonesian greeting.

"Oh Ita," I groaned, "I don't think the street leader's wife likes foreigners. I finally got up the courage to speak to her, to offer her a ride home on my motorcycle, but she refused."

"Ohhhh," Ita said as she nodded.

When she made that long "O" sound, it meant she was thinking of a response I would understand. Ita was so patient and gifted like that. After two years together, I often thought that we could go on a game show together and win big money because she was so adept at deciphering my broken speech, and putting hers into terms I could comprehend.

"What did you say to her?" Ita finally asked, feeling certain that I had come to the wrong conclusion about the street leader's wife's prejudice against foreigners.

"Well, I simply greeted her, saying, 'Good afternoon.' Then I offered to give her a ride home. I could see she was unsure about it, so I assured her I knew how to 'bencong'."

"You told her you know how to bencong?" she asked, looking startled. I nodded,

"Yes, you know, it means to give someone a ride on the back of one's motorcycle."

I felt really silly describing Indonesian vocabulary to my Indonesian friend. Ita burst into gales of laughter and only upon catching her breath did she bring clarity to the misunderstanding.

"Bi, to give someone a ride on your motorcycle is to bonceng," she explained. "Bencong means transvestite or cross dresser!" she blurted out, barely able to say it before excusing herself to use the restroom to keep from wetting herself.

Even as she half ran and half hopped away, I heard Ita's voice trailing off,

"Bi said 'bencong' to the street leader's wife! Oh have mercy…"

Frozen with humiliation, I consoled myself that at some point I'd find this as humorous as Ita found it then. I guessed I knew who wouldn't be invited to any upcoming tea parties at the street leader's house.

Lessons for the Traveler:

1. Language bloopers happen. They are embarrassing, but not the end of the world. They'll be funny after the humiliation passes.

2. Devout women do not feel inclined to ride on motorcycles with self professed cross dressers.

3. Having local friends to laugh *with* you and help you understand your language errors is a wonderful gift. When confused by a response, review the scenerio with a trusted

friend.

13

Powerful Phrases
and Polite Company

Every language learner knows that the first key to success is LISTENING closely to the sounds and rhythm of the desired language, and the second is trying to imitate natural speech patterns as accurately as possible. The method of learning language directly from the general public, however, carries with it inherent danger. One such danger is picking up phrases that might be commonly used, but aren't really for "polite company." The new user of such phrases might not know the precise meaning of the words, but only the response they incite, be it a laugh or a gasp.

In my case, I learned a phrase used to stop unwanted behavior. Ita used said phrase on her kids when they were naughty, and boy, was it effective! All four of them would stop dead in their tracks upon hearing it. Literally, the words simply meant, "Less than learned," so I figured it must be the equivalent of "ignoramus." I was surprised by the level of offense such simple words carried, but just attributed it to low self esteem; people not wanting to be thought uneducated. I did notice that the use of the phrase always came after repeated warnings and heightened irritation, so I knew it was potent. I made mental note of this strong rebuke, so I'd be able to whip it out in the unlikely event that anyone would ever address me in a threatening manner.

One morning, I found myself in need of this verbal repellant when a smarmy man approached me in the fish market downtown. He did not have the gracious manner of most Indonesians I'd met. He did not engage me in the usual barrage of personal questions, but instead went directly to suggestive, inappropriate speech. Without raising my voice, I simply said to the man in indonesian,

"Well, I can see that you are 'less than learned!'" of course using the wonderful phrase I had heard.

He stopped short of a reply, eyes wide, mouth gaping, turned on his heels, and hastened away. I was thrilled! *So* proud of myself. I felt like John Wayne, blowing the smoke off the point of his pistol and returning it to his holster. I mean, who needed mace when I had *creep off* in the form of a simple little phrase?

I could hardly wait to report this great victory to Lisa and share this secret weapon with her. Who knew but that she might one day need this nugget of verbal gold to fend off would be assailants? I was delighted to find Lisa and her best friend Mawarni there at the house, chatting on the sofa.

"Hey, guess what?" I exclaimed upon entry. "This awful man bothered me in the fish market downtown and all I had to do to get him to leave me alone was say 'I can see you are less than learned.' And he backed right off!"

"Wow, that's great!" Lisa acknowledged, impressed, "How did you know to say that? I've never heard that phrase before."

Truly impressed, as I knew she would be, she asked me to repeat the phrase again slowly so she could commit it to memory. Before I could say it again, Mawarni stopped me cold, not the least bit amused.

"Oh, Alice, never, ever say that to somebody! Polite people don't talk like that. That phrase is very, very bad here. WHERE did you hear that?"

Dashed, and a touch embarrassed, I mumbled,

"Well, sometimes times if Ita's kids are really naughty…" at which point she cut me off muttering Arabic words of shock and dismay.

"How bad could it be, 'less than learned'?" I continued, slow to release my new weapon.

"Yeah, and it worked!" Lisa chimed in.

"Oh, have mercy! The point is, don't say it again!" Mawarni scolded, followed by a mini lecture on mannerly speech of adult women in society.

I asked how I could put such a satisfying and hasty end to unwanted attention, and she simply recommended I find other more creative, less vulgar ways to do so. When I went to Ita's to find solace, she was horrified when I told her what I'd said.

"Bi! Oh, Bibi! You didn't actually SAY that to someone, did you? Where in the world did you learn such dirty language? Never, ever say that again!"

"Well… I heard it here, from you, when the kids were being naughty." I peeped, ashamed of both of us.

Shocked, silent, mortified, Ita just stared at me for a moment, realizing her role in the scandal.

"Bi," she said softly and seriously, "You can't understand because you don't have children, but sometimes they make us so upset we don't realize what we're saying. For you, however, you must not do as I do, but rather do as I say do. Ask me before carelessly slinging words around when you don't know what they mean, okay?"

So, I learned yet another lesson about language learning barefoot style as opposed to learning in a classroom. To this day, however, I feel great satisfaction when I remember the way that smarmy man's face dropped when I bowled him over with my verbal mace. My fingers still spontaneously form into little John Wayne pistols, smoking after making the world a safer place.

Lessons for the Traveler:

1. Double check new phrases with close friends before using them in public.

2. The "Do as I SAY, not as I do!" concept knows no cultural bounds.

3. There are many effective strategies for saving oneself from annoying strangers, but cursing at them shouldn't be one of them. Pretending not to hear and walking away almost always does the trick.

14

The Human Blender

Amongst the myriad of reasons my Indonesian friends wondered and worried about me was the phenomenon that I didn't cook. Being single past 30 was scandalous enough, though not as much of a mystery, but what kind of adult woman doesn't cook? In their panic to find me a husband at my advanced age, my Indonesian friends never told me to lose weight or try to pretty myself up a bit (although that did get an occasional mention from the bravest ones). No, my most severe and glaring handicap in finding a spouse, they declared, was my inability to cook. Older women would just throw up their hands in disgust and decry the evil of overeducating girls with meaningless degrees.

I did find, however, that one of the best ways to spend quality time with my friend Ita was to join her in some of her home making duties. She wouldn't let me touch the laundry except to help her fold it when it was already clean, but she would let me function as a blender when she was cooking. The traditional way of grinding spices in Indonesia is to have a large stone, which can be rectangular or circular in shape, upon which the spices in their natural forms are placed. Then, using a smaller stone, which may be cylindrical or round according to the shape of the bottom stone, one grinds the spices together into a thick paste. That mashed concoction is then added to whatever is cooking in the wok. I would name the spices, but I only knew them as *orange root, beige root,* and *little round balls,* along with red chili peppers and little green hot peppers. There were other recognizable ingredients, too, like tomatoes and garlic to squash into the mix.

Ita often used coconut milk, the processing of which involved taking a brown coconut to the corner to have the man with the special machine cut the coconut shavings out of the shell for her. He had a whirling steel rod with sharp edges near the end of it that would strip the white coconut meat right from the shell into a bucket. Then, Ita would bring back the shavings and squeeze the coconut milk out of them. She would throw the remaining dehydrated shavings in the trash.

My job was to sit on the low stool next to the rectangular big stone and wait for Ita to put the various ingredients on the flat center of it. I would then lean over, hold the cylindrical stone with both hands, and rock back and forth, mashing the various ingredients together and being careful not to touch any of the food with my hands.

After months of being Ita's blender, there were certain foods I felt confident I could make myself. After all, I saw the ingredients. I saw what Ita did. I could grind everything together myself, accomplished blender that I was. How hard could it be? I didn't mention my cooking experiment to anyone ahead of time because I didn't want an audience correcting me every step of the process. I wanted to surprise everyone, to silence their mocking voices about my inability to cook.

One afternoon, after Lisa and her friend Mawarni had left the house, I sneaked into the kitchen with my ingredients. I still hadn't learned how to clean fish properly, so I thought I'd try to cook some vegetables (read: leaves) for my first trial. I did the part I best understood first, blending the ingredients together on our big stone. Then all I needed was to squeeze the coconut milk out of the coconut shavings, and I'd be ready to heat up the automatic eye of the stove. I washed my hands again and grabbed a big bowl, not sure just how much milk the shavings from a sandwich sized plastic bag would yield, but remembering Ita had always accumulated plenty.

I took a handful of the coconut shavings in my right hand (not my left, which in Muslim cultures is considered unclean) and squeezed. I squeezed and I squeezed. I squished, scrunched, and squashed those shavings with all the strength in my body, but nothing came out. I wrenched, wrung, mashed and mushed those shavings until my face was beet red and my clothes were drenched with sweat. And I was also livid. I battled not to holler curse words or throw silverware. How could it be SO hard? I had seen Ita do it a hundred times. "Now I know why children here cry when their mothers pinch them! They must have vice grips for hands!" I marveled. Just then, Mawarni and Lisa came in through the kitchen door to find me utterly exasperated. Mawarni looked alarmed,

"What's the matter? You look like you've been fighting!" she cried, with genuine concern.

In a near tantrum, I described my plan and how it had failed and how I never wanted to cook again, and how I was going to throw all of the ingredients into the garbage because it just wouldn't work. Mawarni looked at the paste of blended ingredients and said that looked fine. She then looked in the bowl with the coconut shavings and asked,

"Where's the water? You need to add water to the shavings to get the milk out."

I remember her question, followed by an awkward silence, but any answer I might have given would have been drowned out by the uproarious laughter that erupted upon realizing what I'd done, or not done, as it were. All I could do in my dilapidated state was resort to my constant comfort in Indonesia: the repetition technique,

"Oh… water… "

Lessons for the Traveler:

1. Learning to cook is more successful if we watch ALL the steps in the process.

2. The oils from touching hot chilies can stay on your hands for hours, so avoid touching eyes after touching chilies.

3. Learning can be tiresome and frustrating, even humiliating, but well worth the effort.

15

Crummy Coach

Two weeks before a volleyball tournament, two of the leader type ladies in the neighborhood asked me to be the one to determine which team members would play in each game. I pleaded with them not to impose such responsibility on me because I knew I would be terrible at it. For one thing, I'm fundamentally a people pleaser, something no good coach can be. And secondly, I was an outsider, therefore the least informed about the skill level, temperaments, and best playing combinations of the various players on our team. The ladies insisted, however, saying that it would be awkward for them because they wouldn't want to offend old friends, but that everyone would respect my neutrality in player selection. Finally, I gave in, but I warned them that I would follow my mother's example when she coached my soccer team in junior high: I'd let everybody play as equal an amount as possible, regardless of skill level, win or lose.

They assured me that that was what they wanted, too, and that fellowship was more important than winning. With that understanding in place, I agreed to be the coach for the day. When the tournament rolled around, I did exactly what

I had said I would: I gave everyone a chance to play as much as possible in the five games we played. If we had open slots after everyone had played, I filled them with the more skillful players. Only three people played up to three games, and I wasn't one of them. One lady asked me why I let Ita play all three games, insinuating that I let her in because she was my best friend. I silenced her by asking,

"Who is sitting out that is a better player than Ita?"

In terms of winning, my noble strategy failed miserably. We lost. We lost badly. I knew my teammates were disappointed, but only a few of them were bold enough to address me. It didn't hurt my feelings, though, because I knew the less skillful players who normally wouldn't have been allowed to play were satisfied.

"Fine," I told complainers light heartedly, "let someone else choose next time, because if I'm the one to choose again, I will surely use the same method."

The night the tournament ended, even Ita expressed her dismay, asking me why I had let one particularly weak player in. I recounted the Betty Crocker philosophy that we were playing for fun and fellowship, not as professionals, thus everyone should play as much as possible. Ita couldn't say anything, really, because we did claim to play for recreation with friends, but she was clearly dissatisfied with the results.

"Next time," Ita advised, "let someone else pick, okay? You think too much."

We laughed and let it go, but in my heart, I knew Betty Crocker's way was right. From Ita's, I went to a neighbor's house, where some of us volleyball girls gathered to watch the movie *Titanic* on laser disc. The movie was in English, but had Indonesian subtitles. Eight ladies and their combined two dozen children chatted throughout the movie. At first, I felt frustrated and confused, thinking, "What's going on here? I can't hear a thing and neither can they. I thought we came here to watch a movie! How can they possibly follow the story, talking every minute like that?" Lisa and I were at a real disadvantage. While we spoke Indonesian adequately to chat with friends, reading was a weak area for both of us. Even the words we did know, when written using their proper prefixes and suffixes, were hardly recognizable. Lisa kept interjecting,

"What did they say?"

If I was fortunate enough to hear a snippet or recognize a word or two, I could help. Otherwise, I shared her confusion. It took every ounce of willpower within me not to shush the crowd so we could hear when finally it dawned on me that our friends had no need to *hear* the movie because they couldn't understand English anyway. They could simply read the dialogue and see the pictures while discussing it.

Lisa and I laughed afterwards and decided we would watch the movie again sometime when we could listen to it, too. I was thankful none of the ladies seemed to harbor resentment towards me because of the losses earlier that day. I did notice, however, that I was never asked to coach again.

Lessons for the Traveler:

1. Regardless of gracious, sportsmanlike rhetoric, most athletic teams prioritize winning.

2. Movie watching becomes an interactive form of

entertainment when the watchers can simply read the subtitles and discuss what's happening rather than listen to the dialogue.

3. Reading subtitles while discussing a movie can become addictive. Do not, repeat, do NOT try this form of interactive movie watching in a Western context.

16

First Bus Ride

Each new experience is rich with opportunity to learn and grow, and to have preposterous things happen. That's how my first bus ride in Indonesia was. No longer was I to be escorted in an air conditioned, smoke free, private vehicle with plenty of legroom and the freedom to stop at will. No, I was to immerse myself in the culture by taking public transportation to my supervisor's house six hours away. Lisa asked our English speaking liaison with the Education Department to accompany us to the bus station so he could make sure I boarded the proper bus. Also, he could establish amongst on lookers that we weren't tourists, but professionals under the local government's care. I wasn't afraid because I'd been in Indonesia long enough to realize that it would be most unlikely for anyone to bother me, especially as a foreign guest. Besides, all I had to do was sit on a bus until I arrived at my destination. How hard could it be?

I was, however, a little worried about communicating since my language was very limited. The bus station was naturally abuzz with multiple buses going many directions, and dozens of hawkers selling snacks and water from stands around the edge of the station or from big bags on their shoulders like peanut sellers at the ballpark. Passengers of all ages and stations in life awaited departure, most accompanied by friends and family members. It was unusual to see lone travelers, or lone anybody, really, in a country with 240 million people for whom community *is* identity.

Other pockets of people milling around were watching for the arrival of passengers they were eager to greet, perhaps relatives visiting from distant cities, flocking home for a wedding or a funeral. Ticket agents from the three major bus lines and their various subsidiaries were scattered about the station, hailing, even chasing, every approaching vehicle, calling out,

"Where are you going? I've got tickets! How many?"

Our local guardian, however, walked past the agents directly to the ticket counter to negotiate a seat for me while Lisa and I endured the usual barrage of questions posed by the growing crowd around us.

"Where are you from? What do you do here? How long have you been here? Where do you live? How long are you planning to stay? Are you married?"

And my personal favorite follow up to my answer that I wasn't married,

"Why not?"

This final question seemed to invite creative answers, but with limited language, I usually shrugged and parroted the answer my neighbors had taught me,

"I haven't met the right person yet."

Our friend returned triumphant from the ticket counter with a special seat for me. He assured me the seat would be perfect for me because it was in the very front, a fold out seat next to the driver's gearbox, in fact. I could literally touch the dashboard and see my reflection unhindered in the expanse of the windshield before me. The big bus had a flat front, too, so I would be close to cars and pedestrians in front of us... very close. It would be like watching one of those IMAX movies about Indonesia, with a front row seat, only I was positioned a good four feet higher than the action. I would also have a wonderful view of the breath taking landscapes as we made our way through the vast rice fields and rolling mountains in the distance. Our friend told me he wanted me to have a seat to myself rather than be smashed against other passengers. Plus, I would be close enough for the driver to watch over me.

What a thoughtful gesture! I was indeed delighted with my special treatment, having a private seat with such an enthralling view, but there was one awkward aspect of sitting in the jump seat, as it was called. Perched up there front and center, each passenger boarding the bus would necessarily come face to face with me before turning down the aisle to find his or her seat. In retrospect, I should have waited until all the other passengers had gotten on before boarding myself, but I was so pleased with my seat, I stayed glued to it. I did, however, feel a little embarrassed to have been awarded the best seat on the bus. Years later, I learned that no thinking person wants to sit in the jump seat because of the extreme vulnerability in the event of an accident.

The scheduled departure time neared and the passengers boarded, one by one. I felt like a greeter at Wal Mart, as I met each person with a friendly, but demure smile, murmuring

"Excuse me!"

Children gawked, no less than their pointing parents, but no one cried or screamed, which I regarded as a good start. I wasn't sure how many seats were on that big bus, but it seemed to me that several dozen people got on. With the passengers loaded, we were ready to pull out of the station and onto the single road that stretched from the northern to the southern end of our province. The driver, positioned just on the other side of the gear shift, did not engage me in conversation, but rather lit up the first of fifteen clove cigarettes he would inhale during our six hour journey.

I hadn't noticed that there were any empty seats on the bus, and frankly couldn't imagine how there could be any, so I was surprised when the bus stopped to pick up more passengers on the side of the road. The new passengers we picked up were mostly men in their early twenties, so rather than repeat my Wal Mart greeter trick, I pretended that I wasn't plunked there at the mouth of the bus and kept my eyes forward. The third time the bus stopped, the young men had to stand in the stairwell of the bus. This prompted me to think they didn't understand the maximum capacity limitations. I wondered how to let these men know that each person should be seated in his or her own seat, with the seat belt securely fastened around the waist for protection in the event of sudden stops or swerves.

I looked back to my right at the driver to see that he was not the least bit concerned about safety procedures. Each new passenger represented a new fare, so if he could have strapped people to the outside of the bus using duct tape, that would have been fine with him. I glanced back to my left, just briefly, catching the eye of a young man seemingly thrilled to see me. Was it my perfume?

"Good afternoon, Miss," he said, in perfect English, smiling broadly, "How are you today?"

"Good afternoon!" I replied, pleasantly surprised by both his polite demeanor and his clear English. "I'm fine, thank you. How are you?"

"I'm fine, too. May I ask where you're from?" He asked, having to speak up to be heard over several men who were standing between where he was scrunched up against the bus door and where I was seated.

"I'm from the United States," I answered, determined to encourage this brave young English speaker.

I knew that to speak English in a public setting often invited mockery and the accusation of showing off or selling out to the west.

"Are you an English teacher? How is it that you speak English so well?"

"Oh, not so well," he stammered. "I want to talk to you. Can I sit there?"

I looked around to figure out where he meant since we were packed like sardines in that bus. Before I had a chance to answer, my new friend was making his way through the crowd, excusing himself politely as he carefully stepped in narrow crevices separating the men standing between us.

"There," he said, pointing to the gear box between the driver and me.

"There?" I peeped, knowing that the only way for him to get to the gear box would be to step over my legs, which were firmly jammed up under the dashboard.

"Yes, please," he said, as he began to lift his left leg, facing me, to make the stride across my body.

I was paralyzed, not so much with fear as with shock and horror. He wasn't really going to try to step over me and perch on that little box for the remaining 4 hours of the trip, was he? Yes. Yes, he was. And he was in that very act of traversing the vast plains of my thighs when his right foot got caught under the foot of one of the passengers standing next to me, causing this little man to lose his balance and plop onto my lap, but the far end of my lap, near my knees. I couldn't look at him nor voice a syllable. My mind was consumed alternating between only two thoughts, "If my father could see me right now, I'd be so dead," and "I'm so glad Lisa's not here with her camera!"

"Oh, sorry, sorry," he exclaimed, terribly embarrassed.

He nudged the man standing on his foot, begging his please to release the trapped right foot beneath him. Finally, after what were perhaps the longest five seconds of my life, he wrangled his foot free and popped with agility onto the gear box, which fit his petite derriere perfectly. I would have hung over that little gear box like a giant mushroom, so it was just as well that I was in the jump seat. For my English speaking friend, the awkwardness of the lap dance moment was then behind us, totally eclipsed by the joy of riding beside a native English speaker for the coming 4 hours. He was grinning from ear to ear. There was nothing to do at that point but introduce myself and let the man practice his English.

I have no recollection of the many and varied topics we must have covered in the following four hours, but I recall the dinner break, when everyone on the bus stepped off to eat and recite the evening prayers. Before disembarking from the the bus, my English speaking friend insisted that I do him the honor of having dinner with him so he could point out the most delicious choices from the plethora of ethnic foods that would be spread across the tables in the restaurant at the bus station. There was nothing unseemly about my eating with him since he did, after all, speak English, and everyone could see that we hadn't boarded the bus as a couple. They would also see us part at the final destination when I got into my supervisor's car and waved goodbye. I was always careful to manage one on one interactions with men carefully so as not to play into the regrettable stereotype that American women are strumpets.

As the bus screeched to a halt at the station, I stepped off the bus before my new friend, and I almost lost sight of him because he was very short. I don't mean he was shorter than I was, because I was taller than everyone. No, I mean that man was not five feet tall! I knew what five feet looked like next to me because that's how tall my sister is. This man with the fine English skills would have come to my sister's nose. It was a little awkward, then, when I turned to find him and he had to tap my arm to indicate that he was right beside me. I followed him into the open air restaurant and took my seat across the table from him.

There were indeed many unfamiliar foods at the table. I recognized the fried chicken and the whole fish right away. Other delectable treats were not so easily identified, like the one with tentacles hanging over the side of the bowl or the glob that looked like grey matter soaking in orange sauce. I was committed to maintaining my personal policy of never asking what something is before eating it, but this friend turned guide was eager to describe the contents of each dish and insist I try the ones particular to that area. The tentacles were quite tasty, if a bit chewy, and became over time one of my favorite dishes.

After the meal, we let the other passengers get back on the bus first before we returned to our front row seats. Night had fallen by then, so the bus no longer stopped to pick up passengers so much as to let riders off as we reached their respective destinations. Some people got off at the smaller bus stations along the way, but most just called out to the driver to pull over when we approached a place on the side of the road near their residence, or from which they could take a pedicab the rest of the way.

By the time our bus finally pulled into the bus terminal in the capital city, my brain was tired from straining to hear my friend over the roar of the bus's engine, and to make out his precise meaning through his still burgeoning English But I felt victorious. How blessed I had been to have had a traveling partner along the way. What were the chances that a person who could speak English well would board that bus that day? I never saw nor heard from that young man again, but his presence, except for the uncomfortable moment on my lap, made my first bus ride a very pleasant experience.

Lessons for the Traveler:

1. Bus stations may seem scary because of the seeming chaos, but most people there are simply traveling,

accompanying travelers, or trying to make a living. While it's wise to remain alert, it's unlikely anyone harbors ill intent.

2. Capacity limits on pubic transportation often do not exist.

3. The jump seat, while offering a spectacular view, is not for the faint of heart.

4. The more authentic experiences you can share with the local people, like in markets and on public transportation, the more rich and endearing your time in the country will be.

17

Tips from Winda

Though I have a reputation for not being stellar with children in general, Ita's children were special. I spent a lot of time with them when we were neighbors, so I came to view them as nieces and nephews. I found myself looking forward to spending time with them. They sometimes surprised me with the depth of emotion they could evoke in my heart. Ita's daughter Winda pulled a doozy on me when she was in the third grade.

In 1999, a sudden outbreak of violence against Chinese people generated fear of escalating and expanding violence, so our supervisor sent his driver to pick Lisa and me up for a meeting at his house in the capital city. We had to decide as a team whether to stay or evacuate in the face of the unrest. The night before we had to leave, I went to tell Ita's children I needed to go away for a few days. I was particularly grieved to tell Winda that I might miss her upcoming birthday. We had shared some important moments, Winda and I. She was the one who taught me how to draw water from a well using a bucket with a rope tied to the handle. It took a special wrist action as the bucket neared the water to make the bucket turn over and hit the water rim first. Otherwise, the bucket would simply float on top of the water all day long. Winda had shown me the wrist maneuver, patiently reviewing and monitoring my progress until I mastered the skill.

"How long will you be gone, Bi," Winda asked, fully aware that her birthday was just five days away.

"I don't know... " I mumbled, looking down.

My face contorted and my chin trembled as I fought back tears. The truth was, if conditions worsened, I didn't know if we'd be back at all. I remembered a trick my friend had shared with me about how to turn attention away from emotion by engaging in a purely cognitive activity like adding figures or spelling backwards. So, I began to spell my name backwards under my breath.

"What are you doing, Bi," Winda inquired, her head cocked to the side.

"Sometimes when I'm afraid I'll start crying, I spell backwards. That helps."

"Oh... " she said, "Well, next time, say A-D-N-I-W"

Forget the spelling, pass the Kleenex.

Lessons for the Traveler:

1. The spelling trick doesn't always work.

2. Sudden flare ups do leave foreigners vulnerable to sudden departures.

18

Bad Wind and Magic Oil

Much ado is made in Indonesia over *masuk angin*, which literally means "enter wind" "or bad air entering." It is named as the culprit to any number of maladies that can attack a person on a daily basis including, but not limited to: stiffness after sleeping, headaches, nausea, knots of pain, and gas (which of course really *is* bad wind). In an effort to avoid bad air entering, people refuse to sit directly in front of a fan and make a point to wear a jacket when riding a motorcycle, even in 90 degree heat. Also, if sitting or lying on the floor, we must be sure to sit on some kind of mat so that we don't *masuk angin* from the bare floor.

I used to laugh about this mysterious malady. Ita would diligently put special eucalyptus oil all over her belly and chest before sleeping and would be sure to coat her babies' bodies with the same after every bath. I soon associated the smell of eucalyptus with bedtime, though I always declined any for myself, explaining that I had plenty of layers to keep that nasty air out.

One particularly stressful day, I went to Ita's for lunch in a state. I can't remember what had me so upset, but Ita ran to get the fan to cool me off, careful to position herself away from its direct airflow. Ita listened attentively as I railed on about the day's frustrations and injustices. In one moment of unbridled anxiety, I bellowed,

"I just want to end it aaaaall!!!" and turned my face to the fan, opening my mouth as wide as I could.

"NO, BI!" Ita screamed and jumped over to me, as if I were running to jump off a cliff.

I burst into gales of laughter, and Ita realized that the last bit of drama there had been a joke.

"Oh, you think that's funny, do you?" she scolded, not the least bit amused.

"Well," I wanted to continue, but couldn't, fully in hysterics at seeing Ita's sincere and frightened response to my fan gag; it gave me the giggles, just like the ones I got sent away from the dinner table for in elementary school and I couldn't stop laughing.

"You know," Ita continued, "I know you don't believe that *masuk angin* is real, but one day you'll learn. And, by the way, I know of a woman who jacked her mouth way open like that while laughing and her jaws got stuck like that. Then it wouldn't be quite so funny, would it?"

Again, I had nothing to say, still fully in the throes of the sillies. I wanted to stop, but it all seemed so preposterous to me… being scared of air. I had a theory that parents had just told their kids that fans would make them sick for financial reasons, not wanting to buy a fan, or, if they already owned one, so kids wouldn't fight over it or drive up the electricity bill running it all the time. Nonetheless, Ita could list account after account of the dangers of *masuk angin*.

Several months later, however, just as Ita had predicted, I learned a little something about bad wind. Ita and I were on a public bus, one of the big air conditioned buses, heading home from the big city, where we had visited her relatives and shopped a bit for the coming holidays. The journey would take six hours total, and we had left about nine in the morning after enjoying a nice traditional bowl of rice and vegetables for breakfast. To this day, I fault the passenger sitting behind us for my scuffle with bad air. If I was indeed infected with bad air, it's because the lady behind me gave me hers. Almost from the moment we pulled away from the curb in the city, she was expelling the most horrendous belches, followed by groans to the woman beside her that she had *masuk angin*.

At first, I chortled to myself about how acceptable it is to burp in Indonesia, so that even ladies can release the nastiest sounds without anyone thinking it rude. In this case, the waiflike granny behind me was on a roll. She had to be eighty years old, dressed in a traditional cloth like a typical villager would wear. Her face bore deep wrinkles from years of hard work in the rice fields. The situation was passable until granny discovered that she was more comfortable leaning forward, which positioned her poisonous fumes spewing mouth directly in the crack between Ita's seat and mine. So, not only was the sound amplified, but there were several times I could smell the noxious gases!

I had taken the public bus many times before and had never had a moment's motion sickness, even when traversing curvy mountain roads. Just three hours into the trip, however, I started to feel sick, like I was going to vomit. A generally hearty person, I hadn't thrown up in years, so I was astonished and confused, thinking it surreal. I said somewhat mystified to Ita,

"I think I'm going to need a plastic bag."

"Oh no," Ita said, handing me a plastic bag and reaching for her purse to get the eucalyptis oil, "Would you like some oil?"

As a joke, I answered,

"Yeah, maybe I would," and immediately emptied my stomach into the plastic bag.

When Indonesians have this nausea problem on the bus, you'd never know because they make not a peep. Yes, we can often hear the preliminary belching, but when the final moment comes, they simply lean forward and essentially spit noiselessly into the bag. Not so with me. I was making all manner of disgusting gagging and coughing noises. I felt embarrassed, knowing that others must find my behavior *so* impolite, but I couldn't help it, unaccustomed as I was to this nausea. But this was one of the great things about traveling with my friend Ita. She was a mother of four, so nothing grossed her out. It was all common place to her. I could have gone to the bathroom in my pants and she wouldn't have thought anything of it. Moms are amazing that way.

"Bi," Ita called from right beside me, having to speak up over my retching, "Here's your oil. Let's put it on your stomach, and a bit around your temples."

I didn't look at her, way too busy wiping my mouth with the loose ends of the scarf I had wrapped over my head. Again, *totally* unacceptable behavior. I simply extended my hand, thinking she would pour the oil into it, but I felt nothing.

"No, I've already got it," Ita said, "Lift up your shirt."

I looked at her, having finished my expulsion exercise, to see that Ita had already poured the oil into her own hand and was ready to apply it.

"What?!" I asked, thinking, "She didn't just tell me to lift my shirt, did she?"

"I said, lift up your shirt," Ita instructed, fully in mother mode. "We need to put this on your stomach."

"Oh, of all the indignities," I mumbled, "Can't you just put it in MY hand?"

"No, I've already got it. Now, lift up your shirt," she said authoritatively.

So, having humiliating visions of this lovely young woman rubbing oil on my somewhat Buddha shaped belly, I obediently lifted my shirt just high enough so passengers across the aisle couldn't sneak a peek, and I looked out the window, thankful that Lisa wasn't there with her camera for this.

Ita reached right under my uplifted shirt, rubbed the magic oil all over my voluminous stomach and sides, then dabbed a bit on my right and left temples. Within three minutes, the nausea and headache were GONE! I couldn't believe it! That eucalyptus oil really have healing power! I marveled and rejoiced, enthusiastically apologizing to Ita for my ignorant mockery in days gone by. Ita was most satisfied by this vindication. To this day, I remain quiet when I hear other Westerners laughing about *masuk angin*.

"Alice! It's not real," they guffaw, noticing that I'm not participating in the jeering.

All I know is, it never hurts to keep a bottle of eucalyptus oil on hand.

Lessons for the Traveler:

1. Eucalyptus oil can be treat many a malady, regardless of cause.

2. Mothers know stuff; everywhere in the world. They do. When in trouble, find a mother and do as she says.

3. That which we mock, we often experience. Be careful what you mock.

19

Functional Phrases and Beyond

One danger language learners often face is the ostensibly kind offer to "trade languages." Many people offered to teach me Indonesian privately in exchange for my teaching them English. It seems like such a noble idea, really, but it almost never works in an informal environment because each learner is more concerned about learning than teaching. It's better to focus on one language at a time. Ita was an ideal friend for me in this respect. Athough she would have liked to have learned English just to know it, she recognized that her need for English was negligible next to my need for Indonesian. She knew that learning her language was essential for me to adapt well and enjoy my experience in her country to the fullest, so she focused on helping me.

There was one occasion, however, a two week period, when learning English became very important to Ita. She begged me to teach her some key expressions, even making a list of them. Ita wasn't interested in grammar nor a vast array of vocabulary. She just wanted to be able to communicate with two special foreigners: my parents. Mom and Dad were coming for a visit and the whole neighborhood was aflutter, but no one was more excited than Ita. She knew I'd have to translate longer conversations, but there were some things she already knew she would want to say, and could learn before they arrived. Ita's list included:

1. How was your trip?
2. Are you tired?
3. Please come to my house.
4. Welcome to my house.
5. Please sit down.
6. Please eat.
7. Please, eat more.
8. Thank you for coming to my house.
9. See you tomorrow.
10. I'll see you in my dreams.
11. Did you sleep well?

A very functional list if I say so myself. All perfectly appropriate verbiage for my parents. Except, of course, for number 10. When Ita read that one off her list, I stopped writing and looked up at her.

"Umm, Ita," I fumbled, "that's kind of an intimate thing to say to someone... especially someone you're meeting for the first time. And saying it to your friend's parents, well, is a bit odd. How about another phrase instead, like 'Sweet dreams'?"

Ita stared at me, unwavering,

"Bi, I want to say 'I'll see you in my dreams,' to Mom. It's what I want to say to her. Are you going to teach it to me or will I ask Lisa?"

Seeing that Ita was resolute on the matter, there was nothing to do but teach her the words, which gave her immense satisfaction.

The next day, I left to pick up my parents. Mom and Dad flew into a city six hours away and Ita had four small children, so she couldn't possibly accompany me to pick them up. Instead, she asked her mother and her uncle, who was a driver by trade, to escort me. After all, they knew the lay of the land and could keep us out of trouble, even though neither one of them spoke a word of English. We enjoyed a wonderful visit and, true to their Indonesian heritage, Ita's mother and uncle greeted my parents warmly and even played cards with them the first two nights we were together, laughing uproariously and making my parents feel like royalty.

My favorite picture from the journey was when I asked Mom and Dad, Ita's mother and uncle, to stand together for a photo. Just before I snapped the shot, Ita's uncle threw his arms around Dad! Yep, the retired Navy captain, epitome of American masculinity. We all just howled with delight, except Dad, of course, who tried to be a good sport but was clearly unnerved. Ita's uncle was a family man himself, just freer with affection.

Sure enough, when we arrived in our neighborhood, Ita and her sister came running down the street to meet us. She was so overcome by her desire to make Mom and Dad feel welcome and at home, Ita fully embraced both of them with a big hug; not the traditional way Indonesians greet people. And Ita wasted no time at all to try out her language.

"Mom, I am Ita! Please come to my house!" she

exclaimed, bubbly with enthusiasm.

"Okay, Honey," Mom beamed, "We'd love to!"

The arrangements were made to eat dinner at Ita's and indeed a veritable feast was set before them. Mom and Dad sat on the floor and ate with their fingers like Ita showed them and thoroughly enjoyed bonding with Ita's family. Ita taught Mom to say, "Delicious" in Indonesian, so Mom thrilled hosts all week repeating that word with utmost fervor. When it came time to go home, Ita hugged my parents again and walked out front with them.

"Thank you for coming to my house, Mom and Dad," she said, perfectly.

"Oh, it was our pleasure!" Mom responded, "Thank you for having us, Honey! It was wonderful!"

"Good night, Mom," Ita added.

"Good night, Sweetie."

"I'll see you in my dreams," Ita intoned sweetly.

Mom, the ever gracious Betty Crocker, was a bit startled at first, her raised eyebrows revealing her thought, "Did she just say what I think she said?" Quickly recovering, a broad smile broke across Mom's face,

"Well, okay, dear." her voice rang out as we turned towards the street to walk home.

Ita had successfully delivered the message she'd had on her heart, and Betty Crocker had received it in exactly the vain in which it was intended, as an expression of utmost affection.

Lessons for the Traveler:

1. Americans have a lot to learn from Asians about how to properly respect elders.

2. Never underestimate the value of games in creating strong bonds, even with limited language.

3. Genuine affection unencumbered by ulterior motive is beautiful and refreshing. Try not to let your own cultural entrapments rob you of the joy of experiencing it.

20

Unexpected Tunes

Lisa and I took great care to demonstrate respect for our neighbors, especially regarding social and religious matters. We were, after all, two of only a handful of Christians living in the entire province, so we understood that playing our praise music loudly would be a source of offense. For that reason, we kept the volume on any music we listened to in the house low. We only ventured to blare music if we were alone in the car with the windows up. One morning, we were surprised to find that our car had been broken into, and our Christian tapes stolen.

It was most unusual for crime to occur in our neighborhood. Our Indonesian friends were embarrassed and upset that "guests" had been victimized. But since the thieves had only taken the stereo and the tapes, and hadn't sabotaged the car, nor tried to break into the house, we considered it a small matter with no harm done. The most disappointing part was that, given the nature of the tapes, we wouldn't be able to replace them locally. We replaced the stereo tape deck with a cheap car radio so that if it disappeared later, we wouldn't incur much loss.

Imagine our amazement the following day when we heard *our* songs being played on a local radio station! Obviously the thieves saw the tunes as just *western* music, not realizing what kind of songs they were. At first we were alarmed, fearing we might get in trouble for propagating our Christian music, but then we realized that the general public's lack of English fluency rendered the songs incomprehensible anyway. So, we enjoyed the irony and the scrumptious blessing of hearing *our* songs wherever we went, all over town.

Lessons for the Traveler:

1. Blessings can come from the most unusual events.

2. Possessions are "just stuff." Try to hold them lightly.

3. Most neighbors will NOT want any offense nor harm to come to you, so remember not to blame them for others' actions.

21

Dropping Ita

Eastern and Western perspectives regarding the unseen world can be drastically different. As visitors in one another's countries, we sometimes have to walk a delicate balance between being respectful to our host culture while not denying our own. Experience teaches us things, though. It's easy to snort about how ridiculous the spirit world is until you see someone's eyes turn yellow and hear an unearthly voice come out of his or her body for example. Or perhaps the admonition to not declare a baby beautiful because it might attract unwanted attention from spirits seems ridiculous. We just have to judge each situation based on what we see and feel in the moment.

One day, I went down to Ita's house after work like usual, but was alarmed to find her writhing on the floor with three of her sister in laws gathered around her. They were standing over Ita, but not touching her or doing anything to be helpful. I rushed right over and asked what was going on. Ita couldn't communicate with me because she was moaning and crying out, with her arms hugging her own torso, in obvious pain. The sister in laws, all older than Ita, were hesitant to tell me what they suspected was the problem, but it became clear when I asked why we didn't take her to the hospital.

"She doesn't need that kind of doctor," they explained. "We have special doctors here to handle this kind of problem."

I was torn between my desire to be culturally sensitive and my far stronger desire to help my friend.

"Well, perhaps we could call some kind of doctor right away. She is suffering," I said as I moved closer to her.

"STOP!" the ladies screamed. "Don't touch her! It could get in you."

They were using vocabulary I couldn't understand, but I got the picture that their diagnosis was that Ita had been taken over by a demon of some sort. Being new to Indonesia, I thought that was nonsense, an opinion that has since changed, I confess. But at the time, I thought that was absurd and overruled all of them, instructing Ita's daughter, Irma, to call a pedicab, because I was taking her to the medical doctor.

"Go ahead, but he won't be able to help her. It's not physical," they chided.

Well, it sure looked physical to me. There were no strange voices coming out of my friend. Her eyes weren't rolling back in her head, and I didn't detect any frothing at the mouth. No, I felt sure this girl had a ruptured appendix or something, not some manner of demonic manifestation. Within just three minutes, I heard Irma call from outside that the pedicab was waiting outside. I can't imagine what made me think the pedicab driver would be chivalrous enough to come in and tote my ailing friend outside for me, but after a brief reality check, I knew what I had to do. No one else was willing to lay a hand on Ita, so I needed to embolden myself to simply scoop Ita off the floor and carry her to the pedicab myself. I felt certain that at the critical moment, I would be empowered with supernatural strength like those women we hear about who are suddenly able to lift cars off their trapped babies.

Adrenaline rushing, I went to where Ita was lying, bent down, and to the sound of a roomful of women gasping, whisked her into my arms and began to carry her back through the house. Even Ita was surprised by this brave move; shocked enough that she stopped groaning and clung to my neck. I was twice her size, but a woman nonetheless; not noted for having excessive upper body strength. I, however, was in full hero mode by then, and felt no fear whatsoever. Well, no fear until I got about halfway through the living room and it occurred to me that 110 pounds was a bit heavier than I'd expected, and perhaps I didn't have the best grip on my ailing friend. Ita, through her own pain, evidently felt my knees crumbling beneath us, thereby having a new reason to cry out along with everyone else in the house.

As if in slow motion, I fell forward, barely able to catapult Ita onto the couch on the way down. It was embarrassing and scary, but my adrenaline was such that there was no stopping me then. I picked myself up off the ground quickly and said,

"Oops, sorry. You okay? Let me try again. Come on," and extended my arms to pick her back up.

"Oh no!" Ita exclaimed, "I think I can make it there myself now."

How about that? Healed! Well, at least healed enough to limp out to the pedicab only leaning on my shoulder. Off we went to the hospital, where they gave her a shot of some kind. After a couple hours of rest, Ita was fine; fine enough to ask,

"Bi, what made you think you could carry me like that?"

"Ita, I didn't know what else to do," I told her blankly, "you're so petite and I'm so big, I just figured, 'How hard could it be?'"

"But it was harder than you thought," Ita added, stating the obvious.

"Well, yes…"

Things got a little fuzzy around then, but in retrospect, that might have been the day I taught her the saying, "It's the thought that counts."

Lessons for the Traveler:

1. There are legitimate cases of demon possession in my opinion, but in the absence of obvious manifestation, like changed eyes and voices, consider physical ailments first!

2. Carrying adult bodies further than two feet is probably best left to people with good upper body strength, or more than one person.

3. In most cases, some help is better than no help.

22

On Choosing Compliments

Some words just don't translate well into other languages, or can take on different meanings culturally that can turn a compliment into an insult. One such example is the way we think about being heavy. A common way to greet a friend whom one hasn't seen in awhile is to say with a smile,

"Wow, you've gained weight."

Indonesians swear up and down to horribly offended Westerners that it's another way of saying,

"You look great! You must be prosperous and happy," because to become thinner would be negative, indicating sickness or sadness.

I heard that explanation many times during eleven years, but each greeting of that particular line felt like a knife in my lapped over gut. Another easily misused word is the Indonesian word, 'lucu' (pronounced loochoo), which can mean funny or cute. The problem comes when a well meaning Indonesian approaches a Westerner's baby and exclaims with glee,

"Your baby is funny!"

I have taken great pains during my career as an English

teacher to explain that *funny* in English can mean that which incites laughter or strange, neither one of which anyone wants to hear to describe their precious bundle of joy. When speaking of babies in Indonesia, on the other hand, we do not say they are beautiful because folklore says it may attract negative attention from the spirit world. Though many highly educated Indonesians would say they don't believe that anymore, it is generally deemed better not to tempt fate. Instead, we should describe a person's baby as ugly or rotten.

I hope Indonesians living in America will not try this with new American friends. I learned another one the hard way. I was carrying Ita's nephew, who was three month's old, when I felt my arms begin to tremor from fatigue. He was a friendly little boy, cute as a button. He looked like a little sumo wrestler with spiked hair. Ita must have noticed my discomfort and asked if I was tired, if perhaps she should carry him for awhile. I felt embarrassed to hand him off to someone half my size, but I confessed that, yes, I was tired because he was heavy.

The little boy's mother swooped right between Ita and me and snatched him from my arms, telling me in no uncertain terms that we do *not* refer to babies as heavy. Ita winced, wondering how I could make such a grievous error, insulting her sister. I never learned what was so offensive about *heavy* for babies, but I stuck to *ugly* and *rotten* from then on.

Lessons for the Traveler:

1. Try not to take comments about one's body personally.

Such remarks are simply a matter of observation and not intended to be hurtful.

2. When in error, apologize immediately and simply confess, "I'm still learning."

3. Listen to others' greetings for babies.

23

On Special Treatment

Mothers insist they do not favor one child over another, but there was something Ita found more laudable in her second daughter, Winda, than in her other children. Whenever she tasted something delicious, Winda would save some to let her mother taste it, too, even if she had to carry it around all day or stash it in a secret place to preserve it. Such a gesture seemed nice to me, but not extraordinary, until the day I had such kindness extended to me.

It was on a bright Saturday afternoon, a wealthy man on our street rented a 48 passenger bus to take the ladies of the neighborhood to his daughter's wedding party at the bridegroom's house. Donning our most beautiful wedding outfits, we loaded the bus and headed off to the party, about 30 minutes away. When we arrived, a huge crowd had already gathered, so my friends were directed to go through the buffet lines outside. I, however, was instructed to enter the main party room where the bride and groom were seated with their esteemed relatives and guests. The affluent mother of the bride spoke English quite well and took great pains to point out the contents of every dish in the elaborate feast, and the meaning of every ritual. I had attended many weddings before, though none so extravagant as that one; but I didn't see anything I hadn't seen before, except perhaps the ostentatious gold necklaces, bracelets and baubles adorning the guests in the room.

My usual wedding strategy was to get in and out in twenty minutes. I would greet the other guests, enjoy the banquet, congratulate and take a picture with the bride and groom, then thank the host on the way out. I had it down to a science. But the host's extensive explanation took a lot of time, so I was unable to run my routine. Ita passed by the front door several times, with increasing urgency, catching my eye and discreetly indicating that the others were ready to go. I knew she wanted me to hurry, but what could I do? The host was focused on me, so I couldn't possibly ask to leave without being rude. The clock ticked and ticked until finally, I was able to express my gratitude for the woman's kind attention, and ask to be excused because my friends were waiting for me outside. She graciously granted my request and I never saw the woman again.

Outside, by the time I boarded the bus, the neighborhood ladies were livid! They were hot and tired and irritated from having to wait an extra forty minutes for me. I apologized profusely and tried to explain that I was trapped, but nothing could allay their icy stares and complaints of how long they'd had to wait for me and how hot they'd been while I was sitting in the lap of luxury. I felt so ashamed and helpless, I plopped down on the seat next to Ita, totally discouraged. Ita then turned to me and recounted how many times she'd told me to hurry and asked why hadn't I come sooner? I felt like crying, repeating only that I hadn't wanted to be rude.

The corners of Ita's mouth then turned up slowly, with a twinkle in her eye, and she put her upturned palm in front of me. On it sat a napkin.

"Look," she said, "I brought you one of the treats from our buffet table. It was scrumptious and I wasn't sure they'd have them inside where you were. It got kind of squished in the napkin while we were waiting, but I bet it's still delicious. Try it, it's for you."

Her face was beaming, not wanting me to miss out on something good. I slowly opened the napkin and saw the misshapen muffin, a mashed lump in the wrinkled napkin. I recognized it as one of the dozens of fancy treats I'd seen spread across the room where I'd sat with the newlyweds and their honored guests. I knew that nothing I'd eaten that day, or perhaps ever before, would be as tasty and satisfying as the treat Ita had saved for me.

Lessons for the Traveler:

1. Your being a foreigner can create inconvenience for your friends. Be as considerate as you can, but realize it's just an unfortunate reality.

2. Sometimes wealthy or powerful people will draw close to you in public settings to gain the status of having a foreign friend, but your true friends are the ones who want to help you even when no one else is looking.

3. The sheer innocence and purity of unadulterated kindness

can take one's breath away.

24

Febri's Shadow Puppet

Ita rarely expressed frustration with me, but one time, I pushed her too far. It all began with one of my famous weak areas, namely, dealing with children. Nothing fills my heart with desperation like the sound of a baby crying. My strategy is to distract the screaming child with a silly face, an interesting toy, keys, anything to make the wailing stop. One evening, Ita's fourteen month old son, Febri, broke into a deafening bawl. I scooped him right up to begin my antics. I tried things I'd seen his mother do, like bounce him on my arm and point out geckos on the walls and ceiling, but nothing quieted the little fella. Then I had a flash of brilliance! I fashioned my fingers to make the shadow puppet of a dog, and cast it onto the wall.

"Look, Febri! A dog," I said, looking towards the wall.

Febri's howl reduced to but a few sniffs and a short gasp of wonder as he followed my gaze. Ita looked up from folding the laundry to see how I'd brought his fit to such a hasty end. When she saw the dog shape on the wall, she grimaced in disapproval because Muslims in our area considered dogs disgusting.

"Oh, a dog," she groaned, "You and that shadow dog. You just love doing that, don't you?"

"What?" I protested, "It's the only one I know. Besides, he loves it! He stopped crying, didn't he?"

Sure enough, Febri's eyes stayed glued to the dog.

"Dog," he repeated, pointing.

My confidence was growing by the second. I had found the secret weapon to slay my most dreaded dragon. I decided to up the ante by making the shadow puppet move and talk, even dance. Febri was thrilled, his joy escalating from giggle to laughter. Going for the gold, I moved the shadow dog to the floor, which quadrupled its size. Febri gasped, silent. "Wow, he's so excited," I thought.

"Here he comes, ruff, ruff," I said as I continued to move the now enormous shadow dog closer.

All of the sudden, Febri convulsed in my arms and shrieked at the top of his lungs. He was terrified! Realizing my error, I immediately put the dog back on the wall, but there was no consoling little Febri. Ita got up from her piles of laundry to remove her screeching son from my arms as she glared at me, grumbling,

"I hope you are satisfied! You and your dog."

Oh dear, note to self about the shadow dog...

Lessons for the Traveler:

1. With few exceptions, dogs and pigs are unwelcome in the Muslim world; so songs, pictures, stories, and images of these animals are unwelcome, too.

2. Sometimes it pays to leave well enough alone.

25

Village on Alert

My first exposure to authentic life in the village, the real village, came when Ita's mother's youngest brother got married. I was flattered that Ita included me. I knew I wouldn't be around any English speakers all week, so this would be a chance to try out my Indonesian with no safety net, and pick up a lot of new vocabulary. Plus, just to be up close and personal in the process behind a wedding would be an immensely enriching cultural experience.

That Wednesday night, I boarded the midnight bus with Ita's siblings and mother, and we headed South. We stumbled off the bus in Medan before dawn, ate some porridge for breakfast at a stall at the bus station, then boarded a smaller local bus towards the village, about an hour and a half from the city. By then, the city was bustling with morning fresh markets in full swing. Traffic became heavier and noisier as the morning wore on, but the further toward the village we rode, the fewer vehicles we saw, mostly motorcycles with people wearing civil service uniforms and bicycles with little children decked out in their school uniforms. The roads went from pavement to hard dry dirt, weaving through rice fields

and rubber tree farms, until we came to a big curve in the
road.

"Pull over!" Ita's mother shouted to the driver over the
cassette blaring Indonesian Golden Oldies.

He swung to the curb, kicking up dust and dirt, and we all
loaded off the bus, checking to be sure we had all our
belongings. Ita's mother paid the driver for all of us, and we
began our half mile jaunt on foot to Granny's house.
Neighbors' heads poked out of the house windows,
bellowing warm greetings to Ita's mother as we passed.

"Long time, no see!" One woman teased, "Here for the
wedding, eh?"

"Yes, we just got in this morning, so we'll take our baths
and visit later, ok?" Ita's mother called back.

"Sure. You get settled in, I'll be down in a bit!" came the
reply.

Excitement was already in the air and the home folk were
filing in. We stayed with Granny, who wasn't really Ita's
biological grandmother, but every elderly woman falls neatly
into the category of *Granny* in Indonesia. Granny's house
had electricity, but only bedroom furniture. Living room
furniture had all been moved out in order to seat more people
on the floor. We couldn't afford to waste the space because
crowds were headed our way. The party wasn't going to be
thrown at Granny's house, but there would be a lot of
preliminary work done there, like chopping up vegetables,
folding hundreds of napkins, and preparing decorated
baskets filled with presents that Ita's family would present to
the bride when her busloads of relatives brought her to town
the morning of the ceremony.

There was not a bathroom in the house, so I bathed outside in a concrete area enclosed by tall slabs of tin. An uncle had hooked up a pulley system for Granny's well, so I simply had to lower the bucket until I heard it splash in the water below, give it a few seconds to fill, and pull the rope on the other side of the pulley to bring the bucket back up. To bathe, I first collected many bucketfuls of water into a larger basin near the well, from which I would dip water with a handled dipper that could hold about a quart of water at a time. I'd rinse off, soap up, and rinse off again by pouring water over myself there in that enclosed area. The sun beat down on my white skin casting a glare to the heavens, I'm sure, but it warmed the water and I felt like a natural woman bathing outside like that.

Granny, aunts, and more than a few cousins expressed concern that I simply wouldn't be able to accomplish the task. So, I literally had to run off all the well wishers so I could take a bath privately. Even then, the grandmother figure, Nenek, continued to holler from inside,

"Seles (that would be me), can you do it? Are you okay out there? Don't fall in the well!"

I drew water from the well to brush my teeth, too, which was harmless as long as I didn't swallow. Even little kids knew not to drink water that hadn't been boiled, though many a sip has been gulped down by thirsty kids playing outside through the ages.

"Our stomachs can take it when we're little," Ita told me with a grin, "but I wouldn't try that now."

I, like every other visitor in the house, slept on the floor in the main room, atop a bamboo mat. We lined up as many bamboo mats as we needed so that no one was in danger of 'taking in bad air' from the 'cold' floor. The nights were cooler than the days, but *cold* seemed a gross overstatement. One of Ita's aunts in particular was a most gregarious person. Everywhere we went on the public bus, she would introduce me to all boarding passengers and immediately report that I could speak Indonesian well. Then, she would turn to me and say, very loudly

"How are you?" to which I would return the one word response that I was fine. Ita's aunt would then turn to the others beaming,

"See?"

The biggest commotion over the weekend, believe it or not, was over the fact that I couldn't have a bowel movement while I was there. How did they know? Well, the first time I felt the urge to go, I asked Ita how to find the special place for that function Naturally, I had seven people trying to give instruction, offering to draw the water for me or accompany me so that I wouldn't be afraid. I assured them that I wasn't afraid, but just needed to know where to go.

So, I drew my bucket of water and carried it with me. When I got to the designated spot, which had a square meter foundation of cement with a ceramic *squatty potty* embedded in it, I knew I was in the right place. I hiked up my cloth and squatted, but my body simply wouldn't go. I think it had to do with the fact that the little privacy barrier surrounding this special place was only about waist high on me, so even squatting, I could see over it. Had anyone walked anywhere within fifty yards, I could have made eye contact with him or her. So, while it's true that no one could see anything necessarily private on my body, it was a most awkward scene, so my body just seized up, I suppose.

Holding strong to my personal rule that if I haven't gone within twenty seconds, I must not have had to go, I arose, and came out with my bucket of water still full. Not emptying the bucket of water, was, unbeknownst to me, like a neon sign to everyone that I hadn't gone, and this was soon big news throughout the village. From that point on, my bowels were *the* news item of the village. People I didn't know would pass and call out to me, asking me if I'd had any success yet. The entire village was involved. After the third day, the village was in crisis on my behalf, convinced that I must be in terrible pain, which I wasn't. I couldn't understand the regular announcements being made over the loudspeaker at the mosque at intermittent times throughout the day, but I felt sure the status of my condition was included.

One night, about a dozen of us were sitting around chatting when a visitor dropped in and excused himself to go "to the back." Ita's mother, who was sitting behind me, interrupted him abruptly, saying,

"Shhh," then whispering, as if I couldn't hear, "Don't mention that. She hasn't been able to go since she got here three days ago!"

"IBU," I scolded, "What are you doing? Stop that. Not everyone needs to know that."

She then informed me that, au contraire, it was important for everyone to know so that they could pity me, join me in my troubles; for what could be worse than suffering alone? Ugh.

I assured them that I felt fine and that there had to be

other things we could discuss, but this was to no avail. When Ita's husband arrived Saturday afternoon, Ita's first words were,

"We've been having a good time, only Alice hasn't been able to have a bowel movement."

Oh have mercy, how was I supposed to look that man in the face after that? Was nothing sacred? I cannot remember the names of all the traditional medicines the aunts made for me to eat, but I do recall eating a lot of papaya during the crisis. I considered going to the back, dumping out the water and returning with a tale of victory, but I didn't want to lie. What was the big deal anyway? Couldn't we turn our attention to the wedding festivities?

The wedding was a splendid success and we came home exhausted from socializing with so many friends and relatives. Our final day in the village fell on the 25th of April, the 3rd anniversary of my ice cream loving grandmother's passing. I always try to eat ice cream on that date. So, when we heard the ding ding bell on the bicycle carrying the ice cream cart, Ita and I ran out to buy ice cream for everyone. As we savored our sweet treats, I shared stories of fun times with Granny B from my childhood. Everyone loves a good story, especially about grandmothers, so it was an extra layer of bond between Ita's relatives and me before our departure back to the real world of work and school.

As we took our leave, every step of the half mile walk back to the big road, my new friends and adopted relatives called out their fondest wishes for my success in the bathroom. How lovely to be remembered in such a personal way.

Lessons for the Traveler:

1. Total immersion experiences are a wonderful gift, so if invited to go with a friend to his or her village, be sure to accept and go with an open, adventurous heart.

2. In the context of family, there is no such thing as a private matter. This is a sign of closeness and acceptance, not idle curiosity or meddling.

3. Bloodlines run far and wide, with minimal distinction between immediate and distant relatives. Everyone is expected to play a role in family functions. Enjoy!

26

Releasing the Singer Within:
Part One

In Indonesia, karaoke is a family event, something to gather loved ones around and do for fun; clean, sober fun. Each person genuinely tries to sing the best he or she can, with everyone else recognizing that some people, naturally, are better singers than others. Indonesians are free spirited and gracious about participative singing, encouraging everyone to lift up his or her voice for enjoyment.

In America, we tend to guard the microphone more carefully. For instance, I grew up categorized as a fine athlete who *also* sang, snicker. I loved to sing, though, and, whenever alone, I would make up songs and belt them out with exuberance. One morning, I was singing to my heart's content while my sister was fixing her hair at the bathroom counter. Dad must have heard the commotion from downstairs because he came bursting into the bathroom, demanding to know why I was crying. My sister turned to him, holding her curling iron to her forehead, and informed him that I was not, in fact, crying, but singing. Such was my legacy as a singer.

Being handed a microphone everywhere I went in Indonesia, then, was a coming out party for my frustrated singer within. My voice quality wasn't any better than it was in the States, but the Indonesian people didn't care because the point of karaoke was being together. Just having an American sing was something of a spectacle. I will confess, however, that although I was asked to step onto the open stage to sing at many weddings, I was never asked for an encore, because even Asian hospitality has its limits. The people are kind, not deaf.

Still, I learned a few tricks to lessen the pain for everyone. One trick I learned, the most important one, was to memorize a few songs in the Indonesian language. Just hearing lyrics to a famous Indonesian song come out of the mouth of an American, however mispronounced and bungled, astounded audiences such that I was afforded about thirty seconds of feeling like a superstar.

"Wow," I heard them saying to one another, "She's singing an Indonesian song! How clever she is! Bravo!"

As the song continued, however, along about the second verse, reality would set in, and the praises would become somewhat tempered,

"Wow, it's great that she knows our songs… her voice isn't that great, but how nice that she is trying to fit in. Isn't this fun? Who'll sing next? Have you sung yet?"

Two particular incidents stand out in my mind that illustrate *reality check* moments for me with respect to my expertise as a singer. The first occurred in August of 1998, when my parents came to visit me for two weeks. One of my English teacher friends was planning to get married, and she actually moved her wedding date so that my parents could attend! And she insisted that I sing a song at her wedding. My parents gasped when I told them.

"Has she ever heard you sing?!" exclaimed my mother, Betty Crocker, exposing her deficiency in the edifying speech category. "Well, honey," she continued, trying to recover, "You do so many things well. Perhaps you could juggle or something."

"No, Mom," I countered, "My friend asked me to sing a song at her wedding, and I have prepared one, two in fact. Ita has agreed to sing with me: a duet in Indonesian and a duet in English. Ita won a city wide singing competition a few years ago, so I think she'll be able to carry me."

"Oh, thank goodness! Yes, tell Ita to sing loud."

"Al," Dad interjected, "This is someone's wedding. There will probably be a lot of people in attendance. Do you think you should sing there?" he asked, desperate to protect the family name, as if anyone even knew the family name.

"Dad, it's different here," I explained. "Everyone sings. It's for the joy of fellowship and community. It's not about individual talent like it is in the States. I will honor my friend by singing at her wedding because it's important to her. I'm singing!"

"Well, alright, dear," he sighed, wagging his head, "I'm sure you know best here."

That was a questionable conclusion to draw, but I honestly felt like I was making the right call on this one. The woman had changed her wedding date so my parents could attend. The least I could do was fulfill her fervent request that I sing a song at her wedding, despite my parents', and my own, truth be known, misgivings.

"So, Lisa will be singing, too, I suspect?" added Mom.

"No, she was asked to sing, too, but she flatly refused. She has a terrible singing voice."

Awkward silence... blink, blink.

"Oh, come on, Mom and Dad! My voice isn't that bad! I've been practicing and I sound alright with Ita. You'll see. Oh, ye of little faith," I scolded.

I was bound and determined to prove to my parents that I had been unduly shut out of a world for which I had passion, if not talent. Ita and I practiced and practiced and even had new dresses sewn for the special occasion. We found appropriate clothes for my mother and father to wear to the wedding, too, and off we went on that auspicious Saturday morning.

My parents were floored by the sights and sounds of my friend's fabulous wedding. The bride had even arranged for two superb English teachers to escort them throughout the festivities so they could get a scene by scene description of all the ceremonies and rituals. The teachers treated my parents like royalty, accompanying them from room to room, pointing out the foods that weren't too spicy for western tongues, and being sure that they had pictures with the bride and groom, and sitting on the wedding platform themselves.

When my big moment came to step onto the stage with Ita, a hush came over the crowd. The guests heard the tune to a familiar Indonesian song, and there was a lovely Indonesian woman standing up there with a mic, but was that a foreigner standing beside her? The music started, and people starting cat calling and applauding in support as Ita and I began to sway to the music. Well, Ita was swaying to the music. I was simply shifting my boxy figure from left to right as best I could in keeping with Ita, certain that a big smile would draw more attention that my inelegant movement. Ita cued me to come in on the first note, and in I came, filled with confidence and enthusiasm. Just as anticipated, the crowd swelled with awe and approval. The Caucasian girl was singing in their language! Even my parents seemed pleasantly surprised, eyebrows raised in disbelief, uncertain smiles inching across their faces.

Ita chimed in for the second verse and the applause nearly drowned out the music entirely because she was a natural. The man playing the keyboard recognized her from her singing days and was thrilled to play for her. In his glee, he extended the song to repeat some parts to keep Ita singing longer. The third verse came around, and it was my turn to sing again, only something mysterious happened. My mic suddenly stopped working. Ita swung her mic over in front of my mouth, but my part was over. She sang and sang, and moved close to me so that we could sing the chorus together, but only Ita's lovely voice echoed through the speakers.

I determined that my best course of action was to become a dancer beside my friend, so I threw off any remaining inhibitions and tried to imitate the dancers I had seen on television. When the song finally ended, the keyboardist insisted that Ita stay on the stage to sing a few more songs, but I was thanked and escorted back into the crowd, where many magnanimous party guests congratulated me on my effort. Mom and Dad also were very encouraging.

"Well, honey, you did it! Way to go! The crowd seemed pleased, too."

Left unstated was the white elephant of the inexplicable equipment failure that rendered my microphone mute at the moment I was to sing into it. I noticed that duets following ours had no trouble with the microphones at all. The debate continues to this day: freak accident or reality check?

Lessons for the Traveler:

1. If a friend truly insists that you sing at his or her wedding, make every effort to do so.

2. Even in the depths of a secluded village, people can recognize talent and the lack thereof.

3. Technical difficulties happen. No need to let that spoil the fun.

27

A Watch for Irma

One of the many delicate matters foreigners face is how to handle giving gifts. Being generally wealthier than the average citizen in one's host country, it's tempting to simply cover needs for people who are struggling financially. Giving away one's own belongings or purchasing gifts for people within the community can also become complicated. My foolishness over the years with respect to this issue had more negative impact than any other behavior. That which was intended as help in a time of need created a damaging ripple effect that I came to deeply regret because of the jealousy and greed it raised in even the sweetest people. There was one occasion, however, that I reflect on with warmth.

One day, I lost my two week old watch while riding to town in a pedicab with Ita and Fajar. I was frustrated inside, but resolved not to show it because, after all, it was just a thing. Still, I knew that I'd go crazy without a watch, so I rode to town on my bike and purchased another. The next morning, when Irma, Ita's oldest child, returned from school, she reported that someone had found my watch, and I could pick it up between 5-6 p.m. I didn't know the place, so I asked Irma if she would go with me. She agreed, as always, because Irma was an obedient, helpful child with a ready smile and an earnest heart.

Like so many young girls in Indonesia, even as a fifth grader, Irma could cook, wash clothes and dishes, run to the market for her mother, and take good care of her younger siblings: feeding, bathing, and dressing them as needed. Such ability is common place in Indonesia, so mothers tend to expect such help from eldest daughters, but I always marveled to see the level of responsibility elementary school aged kids, particularly girls, could handle without batting an eye. The children still had time to play and study, but they were extremely competent in household matters, too. Irma was one of these excellent daughters.

When five thirty came, Irma and I went to get the watch. We took my bike, so Irma sat on the little cushioned seat that her uncle had fashioned behind my seat for that very purpose. As Irma and I were peddling home, I opened conversation with Irma slowly, so as to be sure Irma understood my broken Indonesian.

"Irma?"

"Ya, Bi?"

"Irma, for the past eight months, I've been watching you."

"Ya?" she replied again, a bit haltingly.

"Every day you help your mother. You look after your little brothers. You wash the dishes. And you rarely talk back to your parents no matter what they ask you to do."

"Ya?" she answered again, sounding relieved and curious.

It's amazing how much can be communicated in a one syllable word simply by changing tones.

"Because of that," I continued, "I want to give you that watch."

Silence. I kept peddling and glanced over my shoulder to see her surprised face.

"This watch?" she asked, holding up the watch with a big grin on her face.

"May I?"

"Yes," I answered, facing forward, "that watch," I finished, trying to call forth my best Marilla voice from *Anne of Green Gables*.

After a moment of silence again, Irma said quietly,

"Thanks, ya?"

"Ya."

We rode the rest of the way home in silence, me smiling, and Irma intermittently sniffling and wiping her eyes. Thus we shared a tender moment we'll always remember. Irma, Irma… what a sweet little girl she was, and what a lovely young woman she became. Who would have guessed that she would become the first female high school student body president in the history of her city, then head off to college to set a new example for her siblings and myriad cousins to follow? How will there ever come a man good enough to ask for her hand in marriage? And who will cry more at her wedding than her Bi?

Lessons for the Traveler:

1. Always check with the child's mother before giving a

child a gift.

2. The smallest affirmations can make a big difference in children's lives, so be sure to acknowledge honorable behavior.

3. A little back seat on a bicycle can facilitate bonding moments with passengers.

28

Language Mastery or Mystery?

People often ask me how long it took me to learn Indonesian. My answer to that changed over time. When I first arrived, I learned using what is known as the barefoot method, meaning I soaked in language and culture directly from my surroundings without official coaching. Yes, I had a phrase book to get me started on the basics, but I didn't sit in a formal classroom for the first year like many new learners do. At the time, I felt the barefoot method would be more than adequate for me because I could simply immerse myself in my community and pick up colloquial language from neighbors and shopkeepers rather than be saddled with formal, dictionary type language that only academicians use. How lucky I was to be free to pick up the language naturally! I would certainly sound like a native Indonesian in no time at all... Or so I thought.

I studied initial phrases and vocabulary from a book I had in the mornings, rehearsed some questions and answers to those same questions, and went out in the afternoons to try out my newfound treasures on whomever I met along the road. By simply hanging around others, I could see how people spoke to one another in context and I would soon be jumping right in. I noticed that if I listened carefully, I could learn to understand more than I could say, but that was both a curse and a blessing for a talkative person like me. There was always a question I wanted to ask or a story I wanted to tell, but I couldn't piece it together in time to articulate it before the subject changed. So I sat and smiled a lot.

Ita seemed to be able to discern when I was tracking or not, which mystified me. Sometimes, when a few ladies were sitting around chatting, Ita would look at me and say,

"Did you get it?"

Embarrassed that she would ask me in front of others, drawing all attention to me, I would almost always answer,

"Got it," without regard for the veracity of that answer.

It was a response well received, and it allowed conversation to continue without distraction. That worked perfectly fine for me until the day, in response to my "Got it," Ita tested me.

"Okay, what did she say?" Ita asked.

She harbored no intentions to be cruel, but simply wanted to make sure I was on board. Ita always seemed to know when I wasn't understanding, because during the times when I really *was* tracking, I would wait eagerly for her to ask me, but she never did. Only when I was completely lost did she use the follow up question. Like a disconnected phone line, my eyes glazed over, and everyone present could almost hear my poor brain, "Boooooooooooop." Then Ita would explain the conversation in words I could understand.

At the end of my two year term, I returned to the States

and applied for another contract. The man from the home office told me that if I was considering a long term career in Indonesia, I would be required to take a year of official language study at a university. In my heart, I scoffed, "I don't think that will be necessary!" but what I actually said aloud was,

"Well, let me take a language placement test first thing when I return, and we'll see what I need."

Beyond a shadow of a doubt, I knew I would dazzle them with my mastery of Indonesian. The instructor would certainly report that I spoke more like an Indonesian than any foreigner she had ever seen. During the six months between terms I resided with my parents in the States and I called Ita once a week, and wrote often, being sure to keep up my excellent language skills. Ita would write me, too, and her letters made perfect sense to me. I understood every word in them and largely followed her sentence structure when I responded.

How impressed the instructor would be, not only with my adept verbal skills, but my advanced ability in writing... Finally, the six months passed and I returned with glee to my beloved home away from home, ready to take the test, receive the praise, and move along to the next teaching assignment. Imagine my surprise when I took the placement test and didn't recognize 80% of the vocabulary. I saw some familiar letters scrunched in between foreign prefixes and suffixes, but the longer sentences were absolute mysteries to me. To my dismay, I failed the test and had to begin with book one, chapter one, learning how to properly introduce myself. During those next few weeks, the world of how various prefixes and suffixes convey different meanings was opened to me. I realized to my shame that when people asked me if I liked volleyball, I had been answering, "Yes, I make volleyball fun," rather than, "Yes, I enjoy volleyball."

There had to be myriad other erroneous sayings I had ingrained into my language habits, but I couldn't bear to look back and examine all of them. I just tried to re enter the information, correctly this time. I wondered why none of my friends had corrected me along the way.

"It's just the way you speak, Bi," Ita explained, "We knew what you meant."

During the three months of intensive coursework, I continued to write Ita letters, describing these amazing developments, things I wasn't sure she knew either. One afternoon, when I made my weekly call , I was surprised, but not particularly edified, to hear her compliment.

"Oh, Bi, I'm so glad you're taking that language course! Your letters are actually starting to make sense now!"

Nine years later, Ita and I were laughing about those silly first years and Ita confided that whenever she feels blue and needs a good laugh, she just pulls out those old letters.

Lessons for the Traveler:

1. The gracious nature of Indonesian people can make us feel that our language is better than it is.

2. It's easy to impress other foreigners with our use of the local language, but it's unlikely a foreigner will ever speak like a native speaker. Clear communication is the goal.

3. Enjoy the learning experience even when it's embarrassing or frustrating, realizing it's simply part of the process. No one expects you to be perfect, except you.

29

Cursing on a Picnic

As teachers, our opportunities to educate are not confined to the classroom. In fact, it's often on class trips, or when we bring in native English speakers for impromptu conversation that we learn the true level of fluency of our students. One afternoon, Lisa and I went on a picnic with about fifteen of our English teachers. While we were out, Lisa accidentally stepped in fecal matter of some kind. When we entered the car, our teachers alertly commented that it smelled like cat excrement.

"Oh," discovered one of them, "It's Lisa. Lisa stepped in cat sh—!"

One lingual characteristic of Indonesian culture is to respond with a long "Ooooooh," followed by repetition of the last couple of words of the speaker to demonstrate understanding. In my case, this glorious pattern of repetition gave to me an extra few seconds to think of what to say next. So, there they went, one after another, chiming in to say,

"Oh, cat sh—."

Lisa and I were both shocked and horrified, but we knew our *ever* so respectful teachers had no idea they were cursing.

Of course, we seized the teaching moment to enlighten them, but I couldn't help but laugh inside. Lisa, a natural leader, took it upon herself to explain that it wasn't good to say that.

"Ooooh...' they took turns saying, in all innocence, "It's not good to say sh—? But that's what it is, right? Sh—," precipitating yet another chorus of foul language.

The teachers *kept* saying it, and we kept shuddering, trying to bring about understanding without embarrassing them. Finally, we told them about the disciplinary method of washing one's mouth out with soap for use of the word "sh—." Aha, they got it! Surely every language and culture has such words. I don't think I know such expressions in Indonesian, but who knows what actually comes out of my mouth half the time?

Lessons for the Traveler:

1. Don't be offended if you hear decent, well educated citizens using foul expressions in English. They probably don't realize the exact meaning or severity of those words.

2. Do not suppose that you are impervious to accidentally using such phrases in their language as well.

3. Friends tell friends when they're using impolite language, rather than just giggling and letting them continue. No matter how funny it is...

30

Ita on Being Single

My being single was a constant source of concern to my Indonesian friends. One day, I was sitting on a little stool in the laundry area behind Ita's house, keeping her company while she washed her family's clothes by hand. We were chatting away, when Ita suddenly blurted out,

"Bi, when you go back to America, I'm going to pray for you that God will bring you a spouse."

Ita and I had spent two years practically joined at the hip, so I thought if anyone could understand my call to singleness, she could. Still, I knew it wasn't a culturally translatable concept, so I started slowly...

"Ita, have you ever thought that God might have plans for some people that are not like the plans for most people?"

She didn't look up as she was scrubbing her clothes, but I could hear her thoughts like my old disconnected phone line mental sound, "Boooooooooooop." Clearly, despite my line of reasoning, she didn't get it. Flustered, I exclaimed,

"Oh Ita, aren't there any people in your society who never get married?!"

Without looking up, she spontaneously replied,

"Well, sure—CRAZY people!"

Realizing immediately what she'd said, she looked up wide eyed, waving her hands,

"But not *you*, Bi!"

Yes, well… keep praying…

Lessons for the Traveler:

1. There is no place in the traditional Muslim's worldview for healthy adults remaining single their whole lives. No need to take objections to singleness personally.

2. Married friends feel certain single friends would be happier and more fulfilled married, even if they are miserable themselves.

3. Some concepts are not culturally adaptable, period.

31

Releasing the Singer Within:
Part Two

One might expect that an intelligent person would hang up her karaoke shoes after the previous wedding / singing debacle. But, for me, there always remained the possibility, however remote, that the suddenly silent microphone had been a legitimate technical flaw and not the deliberate, unflattering editorial that some suspected. When I was invited to attend the graduation ceremonies of two different high schools on the same day, I knew I'd better be armed with songs to sing. Ita helped me prepare a popular Indonesian song, geared to a younger crowd. She couldn't go with me this time because it was business more than social. Upon Ita's recommendation, I memorized the famous song, but wrote a little notecard for myself just in case nervousness erased my memory in the critical moment. I shoved the security card in my pocket and off I went to the first ceremony at the vocational school in the heart of town.

Almost as soon as I arrived and greeted the people I knew, I heard my name called over the microphone, asking me to take the stage and sing. "Here we go," I thought, egged on by the cheering audience. I bound up to the stage, smiling, and went over to the keyboard player.

"What song, Sis?" he asked.

"Terlena, please," I answered with a satisfied grin, knowing Terlena was the name of a very popular song at that time.

"Terlena?!" he repeated, in utter shock. "That's an Indonesian song!"

"Yes, I know. Let's try it!" I said, slipped my hand into my pocket and cupped the little notecard with the lyrics in my hand, just in case I needed it.

Still taken aback, he launched into the introduction of the song and the crowd roared! The students were screaming with delight and the teachers were cheering. The parents just looked surprised. When I hit those first three notes, the audience jumped to their feet! I felt like a star! I was on cloud nine! I knew I could do it! Everyone was singing, and one English teacher friend arose and came to the stage to dance, bringing many others with her. The cheering crescendoed and I just kept singing and smiling, basking in my newfound stardom. Yes! Finally! I didn't even have to look at my card. It was perfect, and the crowd was still applauding when I stepped off the stage. The teachers greeted me enthusiastically and praised my performance. I had knocked their socks off! Before I wore out my welcome, still on a high, I excused myself to rush off to attend the second graduation ceremony.

I grinned on my motorcycle all the way to the other school, also a vocational school, not far from my house. Several of my neighbors' children attended this local school.

When I ran up from the parking lot, my English teacher friends from that school asked me where I'd been that I was so late. I started to explain that I'd just come from another school, but before I could finish my first sentence, I heard my name being called over the microphone, requesting that I sing.

"Go, go, go!" the teachers urged, "We'll talk later."

Still beaming from the success at the first school, I didn't hesitate to run up onto the stage, and over to the keyboard.

"What song, Sis?" he asked, just like the other musician had.

"Terlena, please," I answered smiling broadly.

"Terlena?!" he repeated, in utter shock. "That's an Indonesian song!"

"Yes, I know. Let's try it!"

As I walked over to the mic, breathless from the excitement, I reached into my pocket to get my card out. It wasn't there. I checked the other pocket, but it wasn't there either. The crowd burst into applause and squeals of elation when they heard the introduction to such a famous song. I was too busy wildly patting down my clothes in desperate search for my card to appreciate their acclaim. The introduction lasted a good minute, so I tried to gather myself, reminding myself that I hadn't needed the card at the other school; I knew the song. All I had to do was relax and *bring it*, just like at the other school. How hard could it be?

The note hit for me to chime in and, as I recall, I did catch the first syllable... and the last syllable of the line. The middle words were lost, but it didn't matter because the crowd was screaming with delight over the song choice.

The next few lines weren't so merciful. For the life of me, I couldn't remember anything except the final syllable of each line. The words, the whole song except those dangling sounds, were gone.

The cheering died down and the music continued to play, but I was deer in headlights up there. From behind the stage, the singer that had come with the keyboard player sang the words, leaving me to lip sync for the remainder of the song, fooling no one. As high as the success at the first school had been, the low at the second school was twice as low. The song seemed to last an eternity, and when it finally, mercifully ended, the audience provided scattered, obligatory applause, but I knew it had been a terrible disaster. I excused myself as soon as I reasonably could, clinging to the hope that it hadn't been as bad as I'd thought it had been. As always, I went directly to Ita's house to report the day's successes and failures, desperately longing for her to salvage the catastrophe at the second school by reminding me that it matters less how skillfully one sings than how desirous one is to honor another's request.

Just as I was beginning to tell my tale, Ita's niece came in. She had been at the second school, so I knew she had seen the whole fiasco. I didn't want her to tell her version first, so I commenced to tell my rendition with full acknowledgment of how awful it had been. How I hoped the niece would chime in with comforting words like,

"Oh, it wasn't that bad. No one even noticed. We were just glad you were there."

Instead, she heartily agreed with everything I said, no matter how overstated I tried to make it.

"That's right! That's exactly what happened! She did that! She didn't even know the words! The singer had to fill in the words from behind the stage! It was *so* embarrassing!"
She made no effort to diminish the humiliation of it all, but rather amplified every painful word in the confession.

Ita listened carefully, wincing, laughing, grimacing, and groaning with each word.

"Oh, Bi... I'm so sorry. How could that happen? We practiced so hard. You knew that song! What happened to the card?"

After recounting the dreadful tale and working through all the emotions of it, Ita brought the day to conclusion with the wise words,

"Oh well, Bi. Maybe public singing isn't for you. Let's just keep it to singing with friends from now on, what do you say? I like to hear you sing."

Ah, so at the end of the day, maybe my American culture wasn't so far out of line after all, relegating me to the has been masses. I can still juggle, though.

Lessons for the Traveler:

1. Not everyone can be a singing star. Fortunately, you don't have to be a great singer to enjoy singing... but perhaps in a private setting.

2. The higher the high, the lower the low... but both pass quickly, and carry potential for learning.

3. A back up note card might be a good idea for public

appearances.

32

Shocking Seamstresses

I had five seamstresses over the course of my eleven years in Indonesia, and three of them have the same name: Cut (pronounced Choot). I knew from the moment I first set foot on Indonesian soil that I would not be buying ready made clothes. Even strolling through malls, sales girls would look at me and immediately shake their head,

"No, nothing for you here."

They weren't being mean, but the *Women's* section in Indonesia begins at about a size 10 in American sizes, so there was nothing big enough for me in any retail store. Given my aversion to shopping, I was relieved at not having to fumble through racks of garments, but I also realized I would need to have some clothes made along the way. The first step was to find appropriate material. Cloth sellers loved me because I bought meters and meters of material. Fortunately, my students, who were English teachers, always presented me with traditional fabric at the end of each class as a parting gift. This was a not so veiled attempt to upgrade my pathetic wardrobe, but I wasn't the least bit offended by it. On the contrary, it saved me time and energy looking through bolts of material that all looked alike to me. With the new fabric in hand, I needed only to find a seamstress to fashion it into outfits for me. My friend Nevi had a friend who was a terrific seamstress, majoring in clothing design, in fact. I knew that Cut would need to take my measurements, which made me nervous, but there was no choice, so I steeled myself to hear her comments.

Even by Indonesian standards, Cut was very petite, under five feet tall. I thought it wise to give her a little warning.

"Cut, I'm a large person, so you're going to see some big numbers on your tape measure. There won't be need for a lot of commentary about that, you know what I mean?"

"Oh, Alice," she said, waving her hand to dismiss my concern, "I'm a seamstress. I see all shapes and sizes, and think nothing of it."

"Well, very good then," I said, pleased by her diplomatic answer, "Go right ahead."

I stood up straight and still as Cut mounted a stool to measure my shoulders and the length from my collar to below my thigh. Sure enough, she said nothing. "My, what an impressive young woman," I thought. "Those had to be twice the numbers she's ever seen, yet she maintained her professional composure." Then she measured my hips. From behind me, I heard,

"Wow!" followed by, "Oh, sorry, sorry."

I laughed and simply affirmed,

"See? Big numbers."

There have been times when I've wished I could read someone's mind. This was not one of those times.

A different Cut, who was older and not quite as petite,

was more mystified by my size than shocked. At one point, I heard from behind me,

"Hmmm…" like she was perplexed.

I'd already given her my standard warning about the enormity of my measurements, so I didn't want to ask, but I was curious.

"What is it, Cut? Are you shocked?" I dead panned.

"Well, I was just thinking how a man here is considered large if his shoulders are 40 centimeters across."

"And?" I grimaced.

"Yours are 44," she stated, peering over her reading glasses.

"Well, thank you for sharing that with me, Cut. I guess that solves the mystery of why I haven't found the man of my dreams here," I responded, peering over mine.

I didn't catch the local language expression she used as she smiled and turned to write the numbers in her book, but I think if I had, I could have learned a new vocabulary word meaning, "Touché."

Lessons for the Traveler:

1. Anyone over 5'6, particularly a woman, is a marvel to many Indonesians. Attention to one's body size is not intended to offend.

2. Having clothes made in Indonesia is convenient and relatively inexpensive because skillful seamstresses and tailors abound.

3. Sales personnel in malls are not inclined to deceive you or pressure you to buy their wares.

33

The Hazards of Rushing

One afternoon, I went to a travel agency to buy airplane tickets, but I couldn't get anyone to serve me. The office didn't have a closed sign, but I stood alone at the counter for a good fifteen minutes, evidently unnoticed. There wasn't a bell to ring nor a number to draw, so I just waited quietly, not wanting to be a demanding ugly American. I tried clearing my throat and going to different parts of the front desk to draw eye contact with someone, anyone in the office, to no avail. Finally, I came to the conclusion that the agency employees ignored me because they were afraid I couldn't speak Indonesian. When merchants in the market had that same fear, they usually rushed to explain,

"I can't speak English."

That afforded me the opportunity to greet them and relieve their distress. In this travel agency, I couldn't even get a look. I went home frustrated, and complained to my housemate and her Indonesian friend that I couldn't get anyone's attention at the travel office. I wondered aloud how the sight of me could incite such an attitude of wanting to avoid me. The Indonesian woman answered thoughtfully that she didn't think they feared my inability to speak the language so much as the way I walk.

"What?!" I asked, honestly befuddled, "Don't I walk like a normal person? What is threatening about the way I walk?"

Looking at me thoughtfully, she explained,

"Well, for one thing, you're always in a hurry, which puts people off before you even arrive. In our view, people who rush are arrogant, viewing themselves as too important to greet and visit with others."

Her assessment set me on my heels, because I hadn't really thought of myself as being in a hurry. On second thought, however, I could see how my hyper focused approach to completing my *To Do* list might have given that impression. Note to self... slow down... you're scaring people.

"And then there's the way you actually move when you walk," she continued.

"The way I move?" I echoed.

"Yeah, you take big steps and your shoulders drop from side to side like this," she said, imitating me, taking long strides and exaggerating movement from left to right the way a burly linebacker or Gomer Pyle might move with that goofy grin on his face.

"Do I walk like that?!" I gasped in horror. "No, I do *not* walk like that! Come on, I have long legs, so the big strides and hurrying I can understand, but the swaying from side to side, no way!"

"I'm telling you, you do walk like that," she said, eyeing me critically. "You asked why the people were afraid and I'm simply telling you. It's the way you walk."

Her tone was so matter of fact, I could see she wasn't trying to offend me, but I could hardly wait to call my friend Ita for an absolute denial on her comments. I excused myself to change clothes and went into my bedroom, closing the door and grabbing my cell phone.

"Hi, Bi," Ita answered in her usual lilt, "How are you?"

"Oh Ita, I'm so offended! You're not going to believe what someone said to me today."

"Uh oh, what happened?" she asked, settling in for what she knew would be a dramatic retelling of the events.

"Well, I went to the travel agency and none of the people would even look at me, much less wait on me, so I came home very irritated."

"Oh, I'm sorry, Bi," Ita consoled.

"And that's not all. When I came home, and complained about it, a girl here told me that the way I walk probably scared them! She said I walk so fast, take big steps, and move from side to side like a big, dumb boy! Can you imagine? How rude!"

"Oh, I'm sorry, Bi," she repeated, stifling a giggle.

"Ita...Ita," I scolded, "Why are you laughing? I don't walk like that, right?"

A moment of silence precluded her response.

"Well..." Ita stumbled, at a loss for words, torn between not wanting to hurt my feelings and taking advantage of a teachable moment.

"Ita, come on..." I persisted, "No, right? I mean, I can see the part about walking too fast and taking big strides, but I have long legs, you know. Those aren't unreasonably long steps for people my height."

"Well, Bi," Ita had made her decision to bring the truth straight to me, "I've never mentioned it before, but a lot of times when we walk together, my thighs burn because you walk so fast."

"Huh? Really? Why didn't you say anything?" I asked, stumped.

"I didn't want to hurt your feelings, and you're always in such a hurry, I figured you had to walk that fast to get everything done," she answered truthfully. "And while we're on the subject, Bi, I really need to talk to you about hurrying, especially with regard to the telephone."

Was she kidding?

"What? The telephone? What do you mean?"

"Well, it's the way when the phone rings, you get a crazed look in your eye, jump up no matter what you're doing, and literally run to the phone. Why do you do that? That's very disturbing to see. I have seen you fall on the floor many times rushing to the phone like that. What's so urgent? Are you worried that someone else is going to beat you to the phone and answer it?!"

Wow, I could tell now that Ita had been wanting to bring that issue up for a long time. I was stunned, unsure of what to say because, as she spoke, I remembered many times when I had been alone in the house, taking a bath, completely soaped up when I heard the phone ring. Just as Ita described, without regard for life or limb, I would sprint out of the bathroom onto the tile floors throughout the house, falling two, sometimes three times on the way, desperately trying to get to the phone. Those were times she hadn't seen. I couldn't count the times she had seen me splatter myself on the tile running to the phone. Ita's words were exactly right! What *was* I so worried about? What *did* I think would happen if I didn't get to the phone before the second ring?

"You know, Ita," I said resolutely, "You are right. I hadn't thought about it before, but you are right. I do run to the phone like a mad woman. I honestly don't know why I do it. Maybe it's because I'm so excited when it rings, thinking it may be family or friends from the U.S. calling."

"Whatever the reason, Bi," Ita said gently, "You should be careful. That's very dangerous. Remember the time I was inside the house sitting on the couch, talking with Lisa and you were outside? When the phone rang, you immediately started running across the bricks and as you crossed in front of the front window, you suddenly disappeared, and I knew you'd fallen. Then you got up and ran the rest of the way into the house; you were scraped and bleeding. Remember?"

I burst out laughing, recalling how embarrassing and painful that had been, and how silly that must have looked from inside the house with me suddenly vanishing from sight.

"Alright, alright," I conceded, "You're right. I'll make a point not to rush to the phone anymore."

"Really, Bi," she urged, delighted, "you promise?"

"I promise."

I decided not to push further about the motion of my shoulders when I walk, making a note to watch that myself when approaching reflecting surfaces like doors and windows. Not racing to the phone would be enough of a challenge for starters.

Lessons for the Traveler:

1. Being in constant haste projects arrogance, an inflated sense of self importance, and is viewed negatively in Eastern cultures.

2. The way we carry ourselves may be found intimidating without our realizing it.

3. Being enslaved to electronic devices is foolish and can be downright dangerous.

34

Dangerous Small Talk

One afternoon, I visited a friend who was a new mother. At one point, she excused herself to nurse the baby, leaving me to visit with her husband in the front room. While we were chatting, the husband's sister came into the living area adjacent to the front room and flipped on the TV to watch an Indian film. Indian films are typically very dramatic, intermittently bursting into extravagantly choreographed musical numbers with dozens of dancers flooding the screen. My friend's sister in law enhanced her viewing experience by cranking the volume up to decibel ten, making our conversation in the adjoining room more challenging. We did the polite thing, pretending not to notice the sudden noisy assault and simply raised our voices accordingly, effectively hollering back and forth to continue our chit chat.

"So, Alice," he bellowed, "Did you teach earlier today?"

"No," I yelled back, "We have a two week break between sessions right now."

"Oh," came the shouted reply, "When you don't teach, do you still get paid?"

Personal financial questions are commonplace in Indonesia, so I felt no sense of offense or intrusion at all.

"Yes," I screamed over an exuberant song on the movie.

"Wow! That's nice," he roared.

"Well, I don't know," I exclaimed, making a lame attempt at humor, "If I don't go to work but still have income, I'm afraid people will think I sell marijuana!"

Unfortunately, at the exact moment I finished saying the word "think" in my clever reply, the electricity suddenly went off, leaving my lone, full volumed voice declaring

"I SELL MARIJUANA!" lingering in the air.

Awkward... blink, blink... The unspoken, but obvious question from my friend's husband was, "Did Alice just yell "I SELL MARIJUANA" at the top of her lungs in my living room?"

I desperately longed to remind him of the context, how it had been a joke, but I just sat there, mute, thinking numbly, "I didn't just yell "I SELL MARIJUANA" in the silence, did I?" I let out a brief nervous laugh and took a sip of my drink before diverting his attention to the ever faithful topic of the weather.

Lessons for the Traveler:

1. There are reasons why Asians don't appreciate loud voices.

2. Trying to be funny comes with risk.

3. Never use the phrase "I sell _____(any illegal substance)" in any context for any reason.

35

Angel in a Uniform

During the year prior to the military operation in my conflict ridden province in Indonesia, I played volleyball for a local women's team. The political climate was heating up in the region, but as long as I didn't involve myself in anything except education and normal life, I had nothing to fear. I was immensely appreciative that no one from either side of the conflict ever addressed me regarding the issues of the conflict, trying to force me to make statements or take sides. I just carried on my life as usual teaching, visiting neighbors, and playing volleyball.

One week, our team was invited to play in a tournament in a city about five hours down the western coastline. My team left in the morning, but I had to teach, so I agreed to hop on public transportation after work, and join them at the hotel, from which we'd go to the tournament together. As agreed, I taught in the morning, then ran home to change clothes and headed to the station for my departure. About two hours down the road, our 15 passnger van was caught in *sweeping*, during which the military checks the identification cards of the driver and passengers, and assures that the vehicle has proper documentation. When I saw the military personnel approaching, I wasn't worried because I had my local driver's license with me. I promptly got it out of my wallet and prepared to show it the officer.

He looked at everyone's cards, then asked me for my passport. I didn't have my passport at the time because it was in the capitol being renewed. But I really should have been carrying a photocopy showing my current permission to be in the country. I had several photocopies of my passport in my desk drawer at home, but had forgotten to bring even one. I felt embarrassed, but still wasn't terribly concerned because I had an active driver's license, a legitimate job and a verifiable volleyball tournament to participate in that afternoon.

I explained to the officer what I'd done, told him I was sorry, and that I had numbers in my cell phone that he was welcome to call to verify my story. He became more and more agitated, insisting that I must carry my passport at all times. He was right. I should have had it, but I didn't, so what did he want me to do? Just as the situation was escalating to the point the soldier was telling me to get out of the van, another soldier called from behind him,

"Hey! I know you! You're that volleyball player! I saw you play last week."

He then looked at the angry soldier and said,

"I know her. I'll handle this," and the angry soldier stalked off, still miffed by my negligence.

When the irritated soldier was out of hearing range, the friendly soldier leaned close to the van and said with concern,

"What are you doing, traveling about the province? Don't

you know it's dangerous here now?"

"Well, I've lived here a long time and I don't feel afraid," I answered truthfully, "I can't imagine that anyone here would bother me. Besides, I'm just going to a volleyball tournament. You're welcome to send someone to make sure that's where I go. We're playing at 5. You want to go?"

"Oh, I can't go," he answered amiably, as if disappointed, "I have to work. But you be careful, okay? It's not safe here right now. I'm glad my term is almost finished. Please pray for me."

I was taken aback by how sincere this young man was, and how he seemed to feel I was his friend when I'd never seen him before.

"Okay, I sure will. Hey, thanks so much for helping me just now. I'm sorry I didn't carry my paperwork like I should have. I will next time, I promise."

He nodded sympathetically,

"No problem. We have to stick together, you know," he said with a smile as he backed away from the van, adding "Don't forget to pray for me, Sis."

"Okay," I agreed. "By the way, what's your name?"

As we pulled away, he pointed to his name badge with a wide grin. It read "EMMANUEL." I gasped to myself. During my five years living in Indonesia, almost every man I'd met had a name like Mahmud or Hamdan, Usman, or plenty of Muhammad's. I had never seen a man bearing the name Emmanuel, a name meaning, "God with us." I tingled from the top of my head to the tip of my toes and relished that encounter throughout the journey. To this day, I wonder who really helped me that day. Emmanuel, indeed...

Lessons for the Traveler:

1. The most unlikely heroes can appear in times of need. This is no accident.

2. ALWAYS carry proper documentation and a spare set of copies. If you are a foreigner, that includes your passport.

3. When dealing with authorities in uniform, remain cooperative. Becoming defensive or belligerent will only exacerbate the problem.

36

Repelling Black Magic

Playing on an sports team is a great way to make friends and to learn closely held beliefs in a culture; beliefs that might not show up in a textbook entry about the country. I learned a piece of privileged information one weekend when I played in a tournament with a local women's volleyball team. The tournament was in another city, so the team had left the night before, but I had to teach a class that morning, so I agreed to join them in progress.

When I arrived, my teammates were jubilant to tell me they'd won the morning game handily. They were, however, very concerned about the opponents we were to face that afternoon.

"That team is from a place famous for black magic," one player confided.

"Oh, black magic," I echoed, in true Indonesian style, "then we'll need to pray before we play, won't we, so God will protect us from any evil forces."

"Well, yes," she affirmed, "But we have a specific way to handle black magic in this case."

"Oh?" I asked, genuinely curious to hear what was next.

"Yes, but before I tell you, I need to say something first. I know you are from the West and what I'm about to say will sound silly to you. But as a matter of respecting us, which I know you want to do, I'm going to ask you to do what we do."

"Well, I'll sure try if I can do it in good conscience," I said.

"We can deflect the effects of black magic by wearing our underwear backwards," she said.

"Wear our underwear backwards?" I asked, surprised, adding, "Won't that give us a wedgie? I don't think we'll be very comfortable playing like that."

"No, not backwards, inside out," she clarified, shaking her head, because the word in Indonesian is the same for both expressions.

"Oh, inside out," I repeated softly. "I'll tell you what I'll do. I believe that God can protect us regardless of what we're wearing, so I can't guarantee I'll do that, but I'll consider it and ask God if He thinks that's necessary."

"Okay, I know you'll do what is right to help us win," she said, as she left the room.

I didn't have to ask God what He thought about that because I already knew. So, I left my underwear on like normal and went out to play without mentioning it again. After the game, my teammate sided up to me and whispered,

"You did it, didn't you?"

"No, I didn't," I replied, smiling, "I just asked God to protect us!"

There we stood, face to face, thinking the same thought

about each other, "Well, I hoped you learned something."

Lessons for the Traveler:

1. "Fitting in" has its limits when it comes to spiritual matters. We can be respectful while remaining true to our own heart and beliefs.

2. Many cultural beliefs violate the religion of the area, but are carried over from the old days. These are taken seriously and shouldn't be mocked even if rejected.

3. Never wear your underwear backwards.

37

Multi Function Undergarments

When good friends ask for favors, it's a joy to help them. Such was the case one day when my friend Nevi called, needing a ride. On this particular day, Nevi and a few of her friends, all majoring in agriculture, needed to attend a meeting to discuss practicum opportunities with a soy bean home industry several miles from the campus, but they didn't have a way there. I agreed to meet them at a bank near the campus at 9:30. I had to borrow my friend's car, which had been borrowed by someone else, so I arranged to pick up the car around 9:00, the morning of Nevi's meeting.

When I went to pick it up, the car was filthy. Not because of anything the users had done, but simply because it had rained for the previous few days and the car was dark green, so it showed dirt badly. In Indonesia, an unwashed car is an absolute disgrace because people who are blessed enough to have a car should keep it spotless. I understood the reason why the car was dirty, but I was embarrassed to go anywhere in that car without washing it first. I was already running late, though, and in a skirt and pumps, so what could I do?

All the way to the campus, I tried to fashion excuses for why I hadn't had the car cleaned before our appointment. When I arrived at the bank, it just so happened that Nevi and her friends weren't there yet. So, I parked and sprang out of the car to see what might be in the back that I could use to at least wipe it off. There was ¼ of a 2 liter bottle of water, but no cloth. What to do?

Then a splendid idea popped into my head! I was wearing a cloth that no one would notice missing should I borrow it for this emergency purpose. I quickly surveyed the scene to make sure no one was watching, and stepped close to the car with the door open to shield me from direct view. I began to shimmy, ever so slightly, to the left and to the right, discreetly working my half slip down over my hips from under my loose fitting black skirt. Just a couple of gentle tugs from outside of the skirt were enough to release my slip to fall freely to the ground.

I casually stepped out of the cotton ring now pooled around my black pumps. I picked it up, folded it, added some water, and proceeded to wipe down at least the top half of the car. Though I tried to look inconspicuous and unhurried, my heart was racing and my hair was sweating under my head scarf. I also tried to remain close enough to the car so that the sun would never be directly behind me and thereby subject unsuspecting onlookers to a shocking silhouette of my less than svelte lower half. My skirt, though long and full, was thin, truly indecent in certain light without a layer underneath.

When Nevi walked up, she greeted me as usual, then commented,

"What are you doing? You look like a real driver, wiping

down the car like that."

"Well, when I picked up the car, it was dirty, so I felt embarrassed to meet you and your friends with it grimy like that."

"Oh, the car looks fine. Hey, it looks like there's lace on the cloth you're using. Didn't you have an old rag?"

"There wasn't one in the car. I couldn't find anything to use."

"Oh, so what is it?" she asked.

Awkward silence... Since Nevi was very familiar with my inclination towards the absurd, a mere glance down towards my skirt was enough to clue her in.

"No!" she gasped, covering her mouth.

"I was desperate, Nev! I'll wash it with Clorox when I go home."

"Oh have mercy... Alice, Alice... the things you do," she said, wagging her head between chortles.

Honestly, I think Nevi was just glad the car looked decent for her friends because it would have been shameful to even ride in such a filthy vehicle. We were both relieved to have the car acceptable in appearance, however unconventional the method to make it so was. I tossed the soiled slip under the driver's seat, ready to meet Nevi's friends with a smile.

I declined to get out of the car again until I got home, where I tossed the grimy slip in with my other laundry. To this day, many years later, that slip has grey streaks faded on it that even full strength Clorox couldn't remove. I have other slips, but that one has great sentimental value for serving so well in my moment of need.

Lessons for the Traveler:

1. Keeping your car clean is important in Indonesia. Inexpensive car washes called doorsmeer are easily accessible in every town to assist in this endeavor.

2. Driving someone in a clean car shows respect for them, like cleaning your house for company.

3. In a pinch, remember ALL your options, even the unconventional ones.

38

For the Love of Durian

The subject of durian is one of the most hotly debated topics among foreigners in Asia. People either love it and can't get enough of it, or hate it, utterly repulsed by the smell of it. There are two ways of describing the smell of durian, depending on who's speaking. For those who love durian, like I do, it is a "fragrant aroma," bringing immediate delight and arousing a salivating effect with but a passing whiff. For those who do not care for durian, words like "stench," "reek," and "disgusting odor" are commonly heard. Durian is literally painful to the touch, being prickly and spikey on the outside, but it is big business in Asia because those who love it will pay a high price for it and go to great lengths to secure some.

One morning I was headed towards the beach, where I had promised to meet one of my college girls and her friends from the veterinarian department. I zipped out there on my motorcycle and on the way I passed a stand with this special fruit, durian. The season had just begun, hooray! So, although expensive, I bought two medium sized durian and told the seller I would pick them up on the way home. On I went to the beach to enjoy a picnic with the college folks. It was very enjoyable, but I must admit I was eager to pick up my durian. I indeed scored my precious fruit on the way home, but I had to play volleyball in just an hour an a half. I knew I had best not eat the fruit before playing because a.) everyone would smell it on me, and b.) I would be burping it while playing, and that wouldn't be a good thing. "Okay, then," I thought excitedly, "I will set it out on the porch behind the house (so as not to smell up the inside of the house), play, then eat it tonight for dinner!"

I went to the volleyball tournament and we didn't end up playing because it was just the opening ceremony, so we were subjected to several torturous dronings by speakers who fancied themselves important, if not interesting. After the speeches, I took a teammate home around 5 pm and thought I could finally enjoy my scrumptious durian! I planned to go home, carry the durian to a neighbor's house, and eat it with them because it seemed a shame to eat such a treat alone.

On the way home however, two of my volleyball teammates passed me on a motorcycle and invited me to go with them to watch some potential opponents play at a location about fifteen minutes away. I went along, knowing that by 7pm at the latest I would be home because that was the official end of the day, with the prayer time that even nominal followers honored.

I was stunned to find that one of the teams playing was a team of transvestites. If these guys wanted to form a team and play in tournaments, that was fine with me, but a *women's* tournament?! Yes, I saw the short skirts and lipstick, but those players were slamming the ball with male strength, even if followed by squeals and giggles and hugs; and it was intimidating, not to mention bizarre. One of the players jumped to spike the ball and an orange, posing as his left breast, fell out onto the court. The crowd went crazy laughing and cheering. A teammate returned it and the orange resumed its left breast position before continuing play. It was kind of silly, I must admit, but the whole scene left me feeling disgruntled.

"I knew it," I complained to myself, "I should have gone straight home. I could be eating durian by now." Just then, one of my friends could see I wasn't thrilled with the situation, so she invited me to have some noodles at a restaurant with her. I realized durian would make better dessert than actual dinner, so I agreed to go along. On the way to the restaurant on my motorcycle, we unexpectedly passed one of the two men she was dating at the time. The one who had serious stalker tendencies. So of course he followed us to the noodle place and joined us. I felt uncomfortable almost to the point of nausea; after all, who wants to be the third wheel, especially when a stalker is involved and durian is waiting at home?

Before we arrived at the noodle place, I had suggested that my friend get off of my motorcycle and join her boyfriend because we could eat another time, but she insisted we should all three eat together. Sadly, I looked at the clock, wishing I could replay the past hour and find myself at home, in warm clothes, eating durian. After the awkward meal, the boyfriend practically begged my friend to let him take her home, but she refused, saying that I was taking her home. Perhaps the other boyfriend would be at her house, who knows? Anyway, we left there, and the rain started pouring on us. I asked her if I could swing by my house to get a rain jacket before heading out to her house. She said that would be fine.

At my house, I ran inside to get my rain poncho, and I had an idea. "I will salvage this miserable afternoon by sharing my durian with this friend and her family!" I joyfully carried the durian out to the motorcycle and asked her if she thought her family would like to help me eat the fruit. She hesitated for a moment, knowing that durian was expensive, but then agreed. Off we rode toward her house, and it was very cold and we were pelted by a downpour of rain. Actually, I was the one being pelted by rain since she had the advantage of my body shielding her from the liquid assault. Perhaps *that* was why she wanted me to take her home rather than the stalker at the noodle place. He was a tall, pencil thin character, unable to offer her much cover. With me in the front, however, she probably didn't realize it was raining. All was well, though, because we had shucked the stalker, and eating the durian was now in sight!

When we arrived at her house, my friend got off the motorcycle, took the durian, and said,

"Well, thanks so much for everything. I'm sorry I inconvenienced you by having you bring me home. I'll see you tomorrow."

Time froze. I was silenced by my horror. Was she walking away with my durian? I felt like releasing a primal scream,

"NOOOOOOO..."

But what could I do? Clearly, I had phrased my invitation

to share the durian incorrectly, making her think I had durian I couldn't eat, so would need help eating it. She would, of course, be mortified to know that she had taken the only two I had. I forced a smile, told her it was my pleasure, and turned my motorcycle around in the huge muddy hole I had inadvertently stopped in during my excitement over finally tasting the delectible durian in the company of friends.

I waved goodbye and watched the door close behind my durian and the person carrying them. I made my way home in the pouring rain. I kept thinking, "I know that did not just happen. How did that happen? What happened?!" Still, despite my frustration, I could see the ironic humor in the whole ordeal; you know, the kind of humor that kicks in after a long time has passed?

To this day, remembering the moment my friend disappeared into her house with my durian, I feel slight pangs of sorrow. The whole day felt like an episode of *I Love Lucy*, complete with the WAAAAAAAAAAHHHHH at the end!

Lessons for the Traveler:

1. There's just a subtle difference between "Help me eat this" and "Help me BY eating this." Best to use the word "together" when inviting someone to a joint venture.

2. Oranges don't make good bra fillers for sporting events.

3. If your mother didn't tell you "there'd be days like this," she was remiss. Some days are just like that.

39

Dangling Ingrid

One dilemma overseas workers face when they return to their country of origin for more than two or three weeks is what to do with their belongings. If there's doubt about returning within a year, one option is to rent a small building designed to have a store downstairs and living quarters upstairs. Such was the case one year when a friend returned to the United States to take care of some personal matters that might take up to two years. Knowing that our Australian friend, Ingrid, had many connections within the community, our friends rented such a space, moved their possessions into it, then gave Ingrid the key, asking her to find someone to keep an eye on their stuff.

Ingrid asked some of her Indonesian friends if they knew of any honest young men looking for work, and it wasn't long before she had a candidate. A quiet young man who'd just moved to the city agreed to make sure nothing happened to the property in exchange for a free place to stay. Ingrid swung by the place every week or so to assure that all was well, and even left her phone number with a neighbor so that she could be contacted in the event of an emergency.

One afternoon, Ingrid received a most distressing call. The neighbor of the storage building alerted her to the fact that late at night, trucks were backing up to the facility and furniture was being carried away. Panicked, Ingrid tried to call the young watchman several times, anxious to hear his explanation. When he wouldn't answer nor return her calls and text messages, Ingrid's fears grew. What if he had sold all of our friend's property and skipped town?! She decided to pop by the storage place several times a day, hoping to catch the young man at home, but she never could. That's when she called me for assistance.

"Oh Alice," she explained, "I'm dreadfully afraid that young man has sold the goods and I will be left holding the bag. How will I explain what happened? I wonder if it's already gone and if there's any point in trying to catch the lad. I really want to just go to that building and peek into the windows over the garage just to see what's in there. It might be completely empty!"

I agreed to go with her to see how we could arrange a look. The windows weren't that high, after all; probably only seven or eight feet off the ground. I thought I might hold the motorcycle still for Ingrid to stand on it and peer in. In our hearts, we hoped to find the young man there at the building, but it turned out we just missed him, for as we pulled into the driveway, he passed us on the street and sped the other direction.

"Oh blast!" exclaimed Ingrid, "That's a sure sign he's doing wrong! He can't even face me! Oh, Alice, what am I going to tell these people about their property?"

I decided to be optimistic, saying

"Well, don't be too discouraged yet. Maybe there's still a lot in there. Here," I instructed, patting the motorcycle seat, "I'll hold the motorcycle still while you stand on and look in the window."

Ingrid looked uncertainly at the motorbike, standing slanted to one side as it rested on its kickstand.

"I don't know... It doesn't look too stable, now, does it?"

"Well, I'll be right here to hold it for you," I reassured her.

"I don't think so, Alice. If I fall from there it's a long way down and that's all we need, me with a broken back. You're tall. Can't you just jump up there and look? Wouldn't take but a second just to see if it's empty."

After considering the impossibility of accomplishing at least a 24 inch leap, I had a great idea.

"I know! Ingrid, I'll bend over and lace my fingers together. You step into my hands with one foot and I'll lift you right up there. You're light and we don't have to lift too high. Just for a second."

She looked incredulous as she pondered the idea with a furrowed brow,

"I don't know. Do you think you could lift me?"

"Oh Ingrid, are you kidding? We used to do this all the time as kids. How hard can it be?"

With that I stood next to the garage door, bent over with my fingers laced together and looked back up at her, encouragingly,

"Come on, girl, right here. Just step right in my hands and I'll lift you up. You can hold onto my shoulder, then grab the window ledge when you get up there."

"Well, if you think we can do it this way," she responded, uncertainly, "will I remove my shoe first?" she asked as she placed her foot into my interlaced fingers.

"Okay, then, whenever you're ready."

How simple it seemed. All I had to do was straighten my legs. So, filled with confidence, I sprung up, just far enough for Ingrid to take hold of the window ledge. But then the unexpected happened. My knees caved. Both of them. They just gave out. There was no pain, no popping, and no strength. I crumbled to the ground, leaving poor Ingrid dangling by her fingertips, kicking her feet, screaming,

"Alice! Alice! Where did you go?"

I was laughing as much out of embarrassment as at the sight of my friend hanging there, calling out to me. I wanted to help her, but I couldn't rise. There was literally no strength in my legs. I certainly didn't want to mock her, but I couldn't do a thing but sit there, apologizing between gales of laughter. It was terrible but what could I do?

"Alice! Alice! It's not funny! How am I going to get down?!" Ingrid wailed. "You're just going to have to let yourself drop, Ingrid. I don't have the strength to get up. It's not that far, you'll be alright."

So, she released her fingers from the ledge and dropped down safely, but not without discomfort.

"Alice! How could I let you talk me into such a ridiculous plan?! I thought you said you could lift me. 'How hard could it be,' you said."

"Yes, yes, you're right. I'm so terribly sorry that happened. I really thought I could do it."

But she wasn't content with that confession.

"Come to think of it, haven't you had a similar thing happen with Ita?" she demanded.

"Oh that... Well, I wasn't going to have to carry you anywhere, just give you a little lift!"

"Shame on you. Will you never learn?" she scolded, exasperated. "But that's beside the point now. I wasn't up there high enough or long enough to see if the place was empty, so here's what we're going to do: I'm going to go get my policeman friend and bring him here. You wait here, hiding behind the building in case that little thief comes back here. If he does, you detain him until I return with my friend."

"Ah, yes," I agreed, "That sounds like a good plan. You won't be long, right?"

"I'll be back as soon as I can get up with my friend. He'll be glad to help and I already told him I might have a problem. You get behind the building and listen for the door opening."

I was game for anything, as long as she forgave me for leaving her dangling like that.

"Will do," I affirmed, as we parted.

So I made my way behind the building and took my position sitting on a tree stump. Sitting alone back there gave me time to think through some contingency plans. As the evening drew on and darkness fell, it occurred to me that I was a woman alone, unarmed, with no transportation, waiting to confront a young male criminal and any associates he might have with him. Did I *want* to hear that door open? Of course just then I heard a motorcycle and a truck pull into the driveway together, followed by the clicking of the lock. The garage door made a grinding sound as it opened. I knew it was time to make an appearance. I decided my best course of action would be to simply act natural and engage them in conversation until Ingrid arrived with the policeman.

Putting on my calmest and friendliest demeanor, I strolled around the building to appear in front of the garage. Two young men were there, stunned to see me.

"Hey, how are you doing?" I asked, knowing that they had no clue who I was, nor what I was doing there.

"Fine. How are you?" they responded automatically. There was nothing truly threatening about these young men. They were just trying to make some extra cash.

"What are you doing?" I asked, keeping up the "I just happened to be in the neighborhood and thought I'd drop by" attitude.

They played along.

"Nothing. Can we help you with something?"

Thankfully, at that very moment I heard Ingrid and the policeman pulling into the driveway behind me on their respective motorcycles. I heard Ingrid firmly reminding him that no one was to get hurt. There would be no "teaching lessons" in violent fashion, she told him. Ingrid, forever the pacifist! After a brief discussion, the policeman told Ingrid and me to wait at the building because he and the young men were going to the houses of all the people they'd sold the property to and collect it back. Yes, right that minute! Evidently the policeman had convinced the young man that it would be in his best interest to remember where every single piece of furniture had been delivered, and get it back to the building before anyone went to bed even if it meant visiting homes all night.

Ingrid and I waited until late into the night, thanfully overseeing the return of the goods. After Ingrid retrieved the keys from the assailant with the promise of no more trouble, we went home. The young men were glad to walk away without severe bodily harm, and the policeman was glad to have been a hero for his friend. We'd all had enough intrigue for one day.

Lessons for the Traveler:

1. Having at least one policeman for a friend is a good thing, especially in another country.

2. Loyalty from friends does not always transfer to "friends of friends." Best to stick with friends you know directly.

3. Many women over 35, no matter how well intentioned, do not have the strength they used to. Think twice before trusting them trust them to lift you.

40

Kickstand Upheaval

The first three months of being displaced from the province I had grown to call home, I was a basket case. I grumbled and murmured about the new location not having anything positive to offer in comparison to *my* province. I fussed about everything from the unfamiliar local language and customs to the traffic and the sweeter food. My beloved province had been declared a conflict zone, so all foreigners were temporarily moved to other regions to avoid any mishaps that could lead to awkward international situations. Initially, we'd been told we must leave for a mere two months, but that turned into fifteen long months of being far from friends who, according to the newspapers, were in constant danger. I hadn't wanted to leave, so I foolishly made up my mind not to like the new area.

One morning in my new, temporary province, as I was running errands on my motorcycle, I got caught in the rain on my way home. I decided to stop and eat some noodles at a little place on the side of the road to wait out the rain. I parked the motorcycle and put the kickstand down as usual,

then started to pull my rain poncho over my head to take
it off because it's impolite to wear a rain jacket inside a dry
area, as it obviously makes the floor wet and dirty, as well as
dangerously slippery. Just as I was pulling the poncho over my
face, I saw that my motorcycle was starting to tip over in the
opposite direction. I impulsively reached out to grab the seat
in order to set it right again before falling when, all of the
sudden, the kickstand hooked my left pant leg, ripped a hole
right through the material, and swept me off of my feet. The
next thing I knew, I was lying flat on my back, with only my
left leg suspended in the air.

Trying not to cause a scene, I said in a commonplace tone
what might well be translated as,

"Oh dear, I seem to be hooked."

The noodle seller ran over and quickly unhooked my torn
pant leg from the wicked kickstand and offered to pour clean
water over my hands to wash them for me. Trying to recover
a modicum of dignity, I congenially commented that it would
be hard to replace the pants because they "just don't seem to
come in my size here," but that the noodles and hot tea might
be just the ticket to lift my spirits, thank you.

I sat in silence, thinking gloomily how par for the course
the humiliating incident had been; how it hadn't rained that
way in my old province and my motorcycle there had
certainly never so viciously attacked me. But then, as I was
midway through my 20 cent noodles, I found myself giggling.
The noodle fellow looked kind of surprised at what must
have seemed like the moment of my slipping over the edge
of insanity.

"You know," I said to him, "in such a moment as that, we

want to be upset because we're embarrassed, but afterwards, we can see the humor in it. It was kind of funny, wasn't it?"

At that, the young, twenty something noodle guy looked down sheepishly and a broad grin slid across his face.

"Well, Miss, actually it *was* kind of funny," he almost whispered.

Then we had a good hearty laugh together. I went home with a hole in my pant leg, but a considerably renewed spirit and definitely a better attitude.

Lessons for the Traveler:

1. Grousing and complaining can come to no good end.

2. Humiliating moments can create opportunities to bond.

41

Tale of a Tumor

Foreigners sometimes lament Indonesians' propensity to comment on one's physical appearance. There are times, though, when their observations could save our lives. One time, when I was living in Yogyakarta, a lump arose on the left side of my neck. The lump didn't hurt, and I felt fine, so I ignored it. I figured it would go away by itself. Several of my Indonesian friends asked me about it, but I assured them it was not a problem because it wasn't painful. I didn't give it any thought until I mentioned it to Ita over the phone.

"A lump?! You have a lump in your neck?!" Ita gasped.

"Yes, but I'm sure it's nothing, it doesn't hurt a bit; nothing to worry about."

The voice on the line was full of concern,

"Biiiii! Oh Bibiiii! Don't you know that lumps that don't hurt can be very serious?!"

"Ita, I'm fine," I tried to reassure her, "I don't even have a cold. If something was wrong, I'd have a fever, or at least feel bad."

But she refused to be consoled.

"I don't care what you say, I'm not going to eat or drink another thing until you have been to the doctor," she wailed.

"Oh have mercy, alright," I conceded, "I'll go to the doctor first thing in the morning, if for nothing else but to prove to you there's nothing wrong."

"Well, alright then," she sniffled, "And you call me as soon as you find out what it is."

The next morning, I went to the doctor as promised. I went to the hospital just down the road from my boarding house and signed in to see an internist. There weren't many other patients there, so within fifteen minutes, the nurse called my name. I entered the doctor's office and sat in the chair across from his desk.

"What seems to be the trouble, Miss?" the doctor asked.

"Well, I have this lump in my throat, but it doesn't hurt. I just want to make sure everything is okay."

"Any fever or other symptoms?"

"No, Sir. I feel fine. I'm sure it's nothing, but my friend said I'd better check."

The doctor arose from his chair and stood behind my chair. He felt the lump, and announced,

"Oh, this is a tumor. It's very large and deep, close to your aorta. We're not prepared to perform such a dangerous operation. You'd better go home to your country immediately."

I couldn't believe he had made such a diagnosis without any tests.

"Don't you think we should at least take an X Ray or some blood or urine tests or something?" I asked, somewhat alarmed.

"Well, we can, but we don't want to waste time. You need to get help soon."

"Perhaps we can at least run a few basic tests while I'm here," I insisted, "I don't want to go all the way home unless it's absolutely necessary. My parents are meeting me here in two weeks for Christmas anyway, so if I'm really that sick, I'll go home with them."

"I wouldn't wait two weeks if I were you," he insisted, "We'll run the tests, but you need to make reservations as soon as possible."

With that bleak counsel, the internist gave me papers to get the usual blood and urine tests, an X ray and an MRI for the following morning. My follow up appointment after the MRI was to be with an ENT specialist. He would be the one to make the call on whether I needed to go home or not. I was like a zombie going through all the tests, numb. Could it be that I was terminally ill and felt fine? On one hand, that would be merciful for me. On the other hand, I was about to ruin my family's Christmas.

When I gathered all my test results, I went home and sat quietly for awhile, reviewing my life. Ita called me every hour to see where I was in the process. While in the hospital, I simply told her I was having tests done. I didn't tell her what the doctor said until I got home that night.

"Well, what did the doctor say, Bi?" she pressed.

Feeling conflicted, I evaded,

"I don't think he knows what he's doing. He made a diagnosis without ever looking at test results. They didn't even take my pulse or blood pressure. How could he have know anything simply by feeling the lump?"

"What did he say, Bi?" she persisted.

"He said he thinks it's a tumor, but I think that's bologna. I'm having an MRI tomorrow morning to see for sure. Then I'll meet with the ENT doctor."

There was dead silence on the phone until I heard Ita's muffled sobs.

"I knew it! And you didn't even want to check," she howled.

"Let's just wait and see, okay? Don't cry. Everything will be alright."

"I just don't want to lose you! I don't know what I'll do," she cried.

I tried to console her the best I could, reminding her that the number of my days on the earth was in the Lord's Hands. We agreed that we should just pray and try to accept the outcome, and we hung up to begin a restless night.

I ruminated on my life: I hadn't really done anything marvelous, but the Lord had been good to me. I had a lot of loved ones and many terrific memories. I dreaded telling my parents and sister the news, though, especially right at Christmas. Finally, though, I could only sigh and release it to the One who knit me together in my mother's womb. If my time was up, my time was up.

I went in for my MRI first thing in the morning. Just as I was lying down in the tube, the internist rode by on his bicycle (yes, some doctors rode bicycles in the hospital to cover more ground, faster).

"You got your ticket yet?" he called out.

"No, not yet, Doc. I think I'll wait and see if I'm sick."

"You'd better buy it today," he advised as he peddled off.

I wondered if that doctor simply disdained foreigners. Why else would he be so eager to send me away? I laid back down in the tube and remained very still until the test was over. Then I took my large envelope filled with test results in it to the ENT's office upstairs.

The ENT doctor's demeanor took me off guard because he seemed utterly thrilled to see me. He had the spotlight on a band around his head, and didn't remove it to talk with me.

"What part of the States are you from? I studied in Los Angeles for a few years and loved it!" he said, bursting with enthusiasm. "I love the way you Americans do business over there, with all the freedom to try new things."

"Really? I'm glad you had a positive experience there," I responded, in chit chat mode.

"Yeah, I was so impressed by the way you people try out new medicines on minority populations before you put them on the market for general use!" he enthused.

Stunned speechless, I just looked him. That was the most derogatory thing I had ever heard about my country and I surely hoped it wasn't true. And the fact that he'd pronounced such an unconscionable practice as a laudable one utterly depleted my confidence in him.

"We should do that here," he added, as he pulled my X rays out of the envelope and put them up to his light box.

Then he looked at the other test results and told me to open my mouth wide so he could look in there. He seemed awfully chipper to be conversing with a woman on her last leg.

"Uh, uh huh..." he mumbled as he flipped his headlight on for a better look. "You don't have a tumor! You have a swollen gland. Three days of antibiotics and you'll be just fine!" He wrote out the prescription, handed to me, and closed with, "It's nice to meet you. Enjoy the rest of your time in Indonesia. Come see me if the swelling isn't gone in three days, but it will be."

He was right. The swelling disappeared the second day. When I told Ita, she wept yet again. I might have cried a bit myself. When I thought my life was finished, I felt thankful that I didn't need to be afraid of death. But when I learned that it wasn't my time to die after all, I was *very* relieved and grateful. The Crockers were going to have a Merry Christmas after all.

Lessons for the Traveler:

1. When it comes to serious medical conditions, ALWAYS get a second opinion.

2. Even when we feel ready to meet our Maker, the thought of dying can be disconcerting.

3. Lack of pain doesn't always guarantee lack of problem.

42

Petty Thieves
and Extra Protection

Indonesia always seemed safe to me. Whether I was in a crowded market, a big city, or in a conflict zone with echoes of bombs and gunfire in the distance, I felt personally safe even when I worried about my friends. There was one time, however, when I had a close call with robbery. I was living in a city teeming with college students from all over the country. I had a lunch date with some friends, and they were going to swing by the parking lot of a hotel near my boarding house to pick me up. For some reason, I was carrying a purse that day instead of the usual marsupial pouch that I wore around my waist despite my fashion conscious friends' protests.

As I sat on a concrete ledge in front of the hotel sign, I held my purse on my lap, not dangling it from my shoulder for some passerby to easily swipe on the run. I was watching the heavy traffic go by when, out of the corner of my eye, I noticed a young man approaching me, from about 2 o'clock, as my father would say. He looked like he wanted to ask me a question, so I looked up, eyebrows raised, ready to be of any help I could for a stranger in those parts.

The young man's eyes locked on mine, but he didn't speak, he just kept coming closer, but at a regular walking pace. When he was near to me, he bent down like he was going to say something, maintaining eye contact, and put both of his hands on my purse to pull it away from me!

I didn't say a word, nor did he, but my two hands were also on my purse, so I just glared at him in defiance and yanked my purse back. He didn't struggle for it, but instead took off running, headed to the main road to hop on the back of his friend's waiting motorcycle. As he ran, he turned back several times to look at me again and again, like *he* was startled by *me*.

I didn't call out to him or say anything, but watched him as they sped away, with him still looking back at me all the while. He wasn't mocking or angry, but seemed genuinely mystified. I heard afterwards that a lot of petty thieves use hypnosis as their weapon, immobilizing victims with their gaze. The way he looked at me, I wondered what he saw. Was he mystified because it didn't work, or did he see someone other than me sitting on that ledge by the time he rode away? He certainly didn't stick around long enough for me to ask him.

Lessons for the Traveler:

1. Beware of strangers who try to sustain unbroken eye contact.

2. Fashion faux pas or not, a waist pack isn't a bad option for

carrying valuables in crowded areas, especially in unfamiliar places.

3. Sometimes there is "protection" we cannot see.

43

Evacuation Decisions

A few weeks following the 9/11 attack on the World Trade Center in 2001, America began retaliatory attacks in Afghanistan. This set off demonstrations in Yogyakarta, the city in Central Java where I lived at the time. Several places around town hosted parades with angry college students carrying signs that read, "Death to America" and burning effigies of George W. Bush and the American flag. Many Americans decided to retire to a less volatile environment until the fury died down. Our company's official policy was to let each person or family decide for themselves whether to stay or go during such flare ups. I asked the owner of my boarding house and a few friends what they thought, because I tend to be oblivious to danger. However disconcerting it was to see my country's flag ablaze, I didn't expect anyone to directly threaten me as an individual.

Every Indonesian I asked assured me I would be in no danger if I stayed, although it would be wise to steer away from raging mobs. Okay, I could do that. I was prepared, then, when I received *the call* from my boss. I saw his name flash on my cell phone and I knew just how to open the conversation,

"Good afternoon! I'm glad to hear from you. I want to affirm our company's policy of allowing each unit to decide for ourselves whether to stay or evacuate. You'll be glad to know I've already checked with local friends and neighborhood leaders, who all support my decision to remain in pocket until this blows over."

After a brief pause I heard,

"Well, Alice, we've decided that all of our personnel in your city will need to be on the first plane to Bali tomorrow morning."

I was undeterred.

"Oh, I understand," came my rebuttal, "For people who want to go, tomorrow's the day. But I know how to handle myself here, so I'm sure I'll be fine."

He, too, was persistent.

"You probably would be fine, but better safe than sorry."

"Oh come on," I reasoned, "Let's say that I did come face to face with an angry mob. I'm a woman, their mothers' age, twice their size, wearing glasses! What are they going to do? Ravage me?"

Pause.

"Well, no... but you need to be on the first plane to Bali tomorrow with your co workers."

He didn't raise his voice, nor lecture me about my naive perspective. He simply restated his directive, case closed.

"Yes, sir," I murmured.

The least he could have done was give assent to the possibility that someone *might* want to ravage me. I made my plane reservations for the following morning, and began to pack my belongings for the journey. The boss had indicated we would return when the situation cooled off, but I feared that we'd be forced to leave, never to return. What was I willing to lose forever?

My birthday had recently passed, and a local artist, Dedy, had given me one of his paintings, with a poem he'd written on the back, so it held great sentimental value for me. I couldn't bear the thought of leaving it behind. Still, it was rather large and would have been cumbersome to carry along with my other bags. So, I called my parents to tell them the devastating news of my evacuation, and to ask their advice regarding the painting. Mom and Dad were relieved that I was leaving with the others rather than remaining alone in the city. I then tearfully described my dilemma regarding my wonderful painting.

"Oh, honey," consoled Mom, "Take it. Take it with you if you can."

"Forget the d--- painting," hollered Dad, "Get out! Get out now!"

Oh have mercy... What did I expect from my high alert, security conscious, control freak, retired military officer father? So, we left the next morning, and I didn't take the painting. I returned a mere two weeks later with much rejoicing, and remained in Yogyakarta for another seven months before returning to my province. We never faced any fallout from the previous weeks' scuffle. There were still dour faced men in long white robes collecting money to "Kill Americans and Zionists," but even those men didn't seem inclined to personally attack us. They were just doing their time collecting funds, as if selling magazine prescriptions for school. I couldn't imagine they gathered too much from college kids, perpetually in need of more funds and capable of giving very little. Life went on as usual.

Lessons for the Traveler:

1. Occasional tense situations do not render Indonesia an unsafe country.

2. Though there are criminals in every country, the vast majority of the population cannot conceive of ill intent towards "guests" in their country.

3. Even a person in the long clothes carrying a box with threatening words on it would be unlikely to attack an individual.

44

Proposal in a Taxi

My Indonesian friends always told me that the best answer to the question of why I was not married was, "I haven't met the right man yet." This response sometimes invited volunteers for the job, which was not as flattering as one might expect. At least it can never said that I haven't had a man propose to me. I've had dozens of offers over the years, some more memorable than others.

I was taking a taxi to the airport one evening, when the driver told me he'd be glad to marry me, but was sure I wouldn't want a man with such a lowly job. Trying to be encouraging to him, I assured him there was nothing wrong with being a taxi driver; it was honest work. This positive reply was met with an invitation to move to the front seat beside him so he could get a better look at me, which I refused, of course. He then confessed that he'd always wanted to marry a foreign woman. When I asked him why, he openly answered that foreign women had a lot of cash. Oh, be still my beating heart, now there's a line to capture a woman's affection.

Deeming himself on a roll and in the running, this taxi driver then shared that when he was not driving taxis, he was a singer for the famous puppet shows in town. Glad to welcome a change in topic, I affirmed such an interesting hobby. This, however, prompted him to commence singing to me in ancient Javanese language, and drive at a snail's pace to be sure he could get in the whole number before we arrived at the airport. I noticed the fleeting time and asked him several times to hurry so that I wouldn't miss my flight. He responded that it would be fortuitous for me to postpone my trip because we could spend more time together. At that, I insisted that he pull over so I could get another cab, but he refused, speeding up.

Evidently, I offended him by so rudely interrupting his serenade and rebuffing his desire to spend time together. He was glad that our relationship hadn't wasted any more of his precious time and energy than it had. The feeling was quite mutual.

Lessons for the Traveler:

1. Be aware that encouraging words to people of the opposite gender can be easily misconstrued.

2. In some cases, one might be wise to pretend not to understand the local language.

45

Wonder Woman
in the Airport

The most wonderful thing happened when I newly arrived in
the big city airport south of my province on April 14th, 2002.
It was finally time to go home after 15 months of
being evacuated to another island because of civil unrest. I
was dreading hauling my enormous bags to a hotel and back
because I thought I had to spend the night in transit. I did
not know an afternoon flight from that city to my town had
been recently added to the schedule. I did wonder, however,
why I saw some people carrying pizza from the capitol to this
city on the plane. I thought how foolish they were because
the pizza certainly wouldn't be any good by the time it got
to our province the following day. Imagine my surprise and
delight when I heard the airport announcer tell passengers
going to my town to please begin boarding.

I looked wide eyed at my bedraggled porter and asked if
he thought there was any way I could get on that flight even
though my ticket was for the next day. He said,

"Well, we can try," as we quickly rolled the heavy laden

cart into the packed check in area, elbowing our way to the front (Lord, forgive me, but it *was*, after all, a matter of cultural adaptation.)

"Sir, is there *any way* I can get on that flight that's leaving in a few minutes? My ticket is for tomorrow, but if there are any seats on that plane, I would just love to go now. What do you say? Can you help me?"

The ticket agent clicked on his computer for a few seconds, then said,

"Well, there are only first class seats left if you want to upgrade."

My mind raced, thinking how embarrassed I would be (not to mention utterly dashed) if I didn't have enough cash on me to cover the upgrade.

"Well . . . how much will it cost?" I asked.

He nodded to another ticket agent to go to the cashier and see. Realizing we were *very* pressed for time, she hopped (yes, hopped, short skirt and all) over the luggage scale and hollered in Charlie's Angels like fashion for me to follow her, and quickly.

So, there we went, sprinting through the crowd, dodging passengers left and right until we got to the cashier's office. The cashier was great with child and looked like she had already been on the job about eight hours too long, so she wasn't as eager to help, but my Wonder Woman agent spurred her along until she click, click, clicked on the calculator and announced that it would cost $13 to upgrade. I squealed with glee, exclaiming triumphantly that we had a deal, much to my agent friend's satisfaction. Again, Wonder Woman waved to me and hollered over her shoulder,

"Come on, let's go," as we weaved stealthily through the crowd.

Well, maybe she was more stealth than I was, but I was lumbering along at a pretty good pace in my own right. When we got back to the exhausted agent with my new, improved ticket, he said,

"You'd better run!"

Then, all of the sudden, I heard Wonder Woman cry out,

"Oh no! You're overweight!"

Okay, that's no surprise to anyone.

"I've had this problem since childhood. Does this really seem like the best time to bring it up?"

Then it occurred to me that, even with the increased luggage allowance executive class passengers get, I still had too much. Once again, like SWAT commandos on the move, we zipped back through the crowd to the cashier's office. I could have sworn I saw one of the fellows in the cashier's office mouth, "Oh no! They're back," but it had to have been my imagination, what with the heightened level of adrenalin coursing through my veins and all.

Wonder Woman ordered them to get the calculator right away, then I gasped,

"Hey, wait. I'm a Frequent Flyer. Does that help?"

Everyone stopped and said in unison,

"Oh, a Frequent Flyer," (in the delicious pattern of repetition that I have come to know and love here in Indonesia) "Ok, then, never mind."

Once again, with Wonder Woman leading the way, we dashed back to the ticket agent one more time, who by then, seemed to be actually pulling for me to make it, like Rocky.

Wonder Woman's parting words were,

"Have a nice flight, Ma'am—now go go GO!"

I could have wept with joy as I slumped into my posh leather seat with tons of leg room, knowing that I would be landing in my beloved province within an hour, and that after having saved at least $100. I don't know when I have ever enjoyed a flight more. And, in my mind, at least, this country birthed yet another female hero—Wonder Woman—May the Lord bless her always.

Lessons for the Traveler:

1. Airport personnel are often willing to bend over backwards to help passengers.

2. Best to sign up for the Frequent Flyer program with your local airline. You never know when extra privileges will come in handy.

3. Flying first class might be more accessible than you think. It never hurts to ask.

46

Close Call
with a Housemate

One Sunday afternoon, my neighbor from across the street came to me with the news that there was an Australian woman in town looking for housing. She wanted to live in our neighborhood, and with a foreigner, so my neighbor felt free to offer up my place, assuring the woman she could live with me since I lived alone. No one would want to live alone, right? Since the Australian woman evidently didn't speak Indonesian, and I knew my neighbor didn't speak English, I wondered how all this communication happened. I should have known right then that any information given was mere conjecture and should be rendered null and void. Anyway, I said that although I wasn't comfortable directly allowing some stranger to live with me, I would be willing to help her find a house.

The plan was for me to call the Australian lady so we could all figure out what to do to help this poor foreigner who didn't know anyone or anything. My neighbor said she wanted to do research for her PhD at the power company, which seemed odd. Nevertheless, I thought there would be no harm in trying to help her, for I certainly knew what it was like to be a foreigner needing a hand. That evening I called her, and we had a nice chat, arranging to meet for lunch Tuesday at noon at a fast food chicken restaurant in town. It turned out that she was an Asian Studies professor from a big university, about my age, maybe a bit older. She had painted red (not orange, but red, like the flag) hair and a silver nose ring. I could receive those things, especially since she had on long sleeves and long pants, and she was very interesting and quite sociable.

We were sitting there in the front window of KFC drinking Pepsi (she's vegetarian), when she mentioned that she did not, in fact, want to live with anyone, because her guests were "sensitive" then, adding that they were activists, in fact.

"Actually," she went on, "I'm writing three books on the political crisis, so I'm not very popular. I'm on a list of subversives, so I can't get permission to be here except as a tourist. The army hassles me, but don't worry, I don't think I'm being followed right now."

I could have passed out. I literally felt like throwing up. The coarser form of the word SHOOT kept running through my mind and everything in me was screaming to run, not walk, from that restaurant right that second. There I sat, in this public place with this high profile politically entangled persona non grata, with my number on her cell phone! Pass the bamboo shoots... She recounted many horrific things that she has found out through her research, and explained why, although the rebels were bad, their story must be told and the army's treachery must be exposed. Just hearing her speak such forbidden words in a public setting made my hair stand on end. This was an *incredibly* sensitive issue, and one NO foreigner had permission to engage in. And I had certainly made it my business to do as I was told, namely stay out of domestic political affairs!

In principle, I couldn't fault her drive to expose the truth about injustices taking place and to bring change. But that's not why I was there and I had *no* interest in being connected with her as it would surely provide a permanent ticket out for me, if not imprisonment. I was just a simple English teacher, quite unintentionally tossed into this precarious situation by a well meaning neighbor who was worried about my being lonely. I went home and just broke down and sobbed right in front of my helper, who comforted me like a champ. She stopped working and sat beside me, holding my arm with a vice grip of shared fear, but commitment to be there for me no matter what. Her eyes were as big as saucers as I described how I'd stumbled into such a terrible mess.

Most of the afternoon, we remained in that state, me sobbing and her silent, but present. She asked me if I wanted her to spend the night so I wouldn't be alone. I declined, but marveled at what a faithful friend she was, really, because she had a lot more to fear from any trouble than I did. Simple people like her disappeared all the time as a result of mere suspicion of involvement in the conflict. I couldn't sleep that night, of course, nor eat for two days (couldn't even binge, true stress!) and in fact spent the following afternoon and evening mostly in bed simply from total physical and emotional exhaustion. I went right to my neighbor when I finished teaching a terrible class and told her who the woman was and what she was *really* doing there, which was not research for a PhD on electricity in Indonesia.

Streams of Arabic spewed from my well meaning neighbor's mouth in her horror that was paramount to my own. After all, her son was a policeman, so that foreigner's contacts would consider him a target, and then everybody's houses could be set aflame. My neighbor didn't try to pretend that there was anything redeemable in either side of the fighting parties; she just wanted to keep safe, as we all did. I told my Indonesian supervisor at work what had happened, and he was also horrified. We agreed to keep it between us unless anything came of it, like an armed person knocking on my door.

My neighbor, it turned out, was related to a recently retired big wig for the military, who still wielded a great deal of influence, so she said not to worry and that if I needed her to, she could help me in a flash. My poor neighbor, she had no idea how awry her attempt to find an American friend a roommate could go. She just went with her instinct to lump all of us foreigners together. Lord willing, that was a powerful lesson for her. I text messaged the Australian woman and told her that I could help her find a house, perhaps, but that I would only have contact with her through neighbor's nephew. Furthermore, I needed her to take my number out of her cell phone because of my situation of working for the government as an English teacher. I couldn't afford to have anyone think I was involved in politics at all. I told her that, although I respected her and wished her well in her search for truth, I simply could not take on the risk of being associated with her.

She wrote back and said that she understood and that she had, in fact, sensed that in me at KFC. I guess she hadn't missed all the color running out of my face when she mentioned her mission there. I wonder if she saw my heart pounding in my chest the way I felt it. Several weeks later, I read about that same woman being taken to jail. I rushed over to my neighbor's house to show her the newspaper article.

"That's her," she gasped, followed by another stream of Arabic.

Those spontaneous Arabic prayers are sure indicators of genuine fear in any good Muslim. The Australian woman was eventually deported to her home country after months of red tape and political jockeying. Proving not all foreigners are alike! Just as I didn't want to be lumped into the same category with other Caucasians and their various agendas in Indonesia, I learned not to look at all foreigners in America with the same eyes as I view criminals from their country or religion on the news. Most people are *just people*, trying to get an education and make a better life for themselves and their children and grandchildren. They worry about staying healthy and making enough money to meet their needs. They like to gather with friends and family to tell stories and eat good food that reminds them of home. Yes, some people are villains with dark agendas, but, statistically, those are few and far between. Most people are just trying to live their lives.

Lessons for the Traveler:

1. Foreigners are known by the company they keep, so best to know another foreigner's business in the country before becoming associated with him or her.

2. Any trouble we get into will reflect badly on local friends even more than on foreign ones.

3. Just as we don't want to be victims of guilt by association, we should avoid doing the same to others.

47

Thrashing Beast:
Fact or Fiction?

During the year I was hosting an English radio program, eight very impressive young professionals visited our fair city and agreed to become special guests for one of our monthly English club's meetings. It was always exciting to have real, native English speakers come, especially young adults, because my English club friends often said,

"Alice, we like you and all, but don't you know any young people?"

We hit the jackpot with the group of young professionals that came that month. We had a computer programmer, a store owner, a lawyer, an accountant, and even a press secretary for a congressman! All of them were well mannered, intelligent, and eager to learn about the people in our area. They showed great initiative experiencing the local food, even spending a few nights in our friends' homes in order to have a more authentic cultural immersion experience.

I was thrilled to introduce these fine young people to my English club. Unfortunately, one of the women from this group fell ill while she was there. What began as a cold blossomed into a raging flu that left her weak from fever. When the others wanted to spend an afternoon visiting one of our legendary beaches, I stayed home with the one who wasn't feeling well. I had her lie down in the master bedroom, closed the door, and worked on some lesson plans in the dining area just outside her door. I told her to call me if she needed anything. Soon, the sun was setting, which meant all the bugs outside would swarm towards the lights in the house if I didn't get the doors shut in time.

Just as I was closing the side door, an enormous moth swooped into the house and went right up to the ceiling. I had seen many moths, but the wingspan on this one was a good six inches wide and its body four inches long. My initial response was to shut the other doors, then return, hoping it had disappeared, but it hadn't. Plan B was to give it my typical verbal warning,

"I don't mind if you're in here, but don't make a nuisance of yourself and *don't* get on me. You just stay up there and everything will be fine."

I don't know why I insisted on trying to bargain with creatures that way. I was forever trying to cut a separate quarters deal with cockroaches, mice, spiders, and flying bugs, even offering the agreement in both Indonesian and English in case they didn't understand my native tongue, but it rarely worked. Okay, so it never worked, but it always seemed worth a try as opposed to immediately shifting into destruction of critter mode. The moth evidently wasn't pleased with its condition either, trapped in the house, so it starting flying around wildly, crashing into the light and the walls and the chairs. Had it been a tiny moth, this behavior would have been annoying, but this gargantuan one practically knocked the light bulbs out of the lamp when it hit.

The ceiling lamp swayed from the abrupt contact, adding an eerie lighting effect to the already unsettling reality of having a crazed monster moth in the room. Against my generally passive nature, I had no choice but to grab the broom and try to help the panic stricken beastie back out the door. I opened the door, doubting any other intruder would be as troublesome as the one I was already facing. Door open, I commenced waving the broom in the frightened moth's general direction. I was attempting to shoo it back towards its access to freedom, but it was already in such a frenzy, it seemed unable to heed my instruction. I then took the more aggressive measure of trying to pin the moth to the wall with the broom, planning to drag it across the wall and flick it out the door.

This was the worst idea yet, because as I extended the broom directly towards the moth, it launched a dive bombing attack on me. It flew directly at my head! I recoiled, ducking, so that it didn't actually hit me, but I felt the whoosh of its enormous wings muss the hair just over my left ear. That narrow miss kicked my fight or flight instinct into high gear and I began chasing that malicious moth all over the house, wildly swinging the broom every way I could. My attacker continued to come back at me from all angles: above, below, right, left, behind, and even head on.

I was knocking things off shelves with the now frenetic broom, toppling chairs, tripping several times myself, landing in a heap on the floor, only to pop up again, sweaty, red faced, heart pounding, and on high alert, white knuckles gripping my bristled weapon. The battle raged on for at least fifteen minutes until I finally struck the winning blow, knocking the assailant right out of the air, then pinning it to the tile floor beneath my trusty broom. All compassion and passivity behind me, I *stomped* on that broom, with power and authority. I guess we found out who was boss in the house after all.

Satisfied, but still gasping for air from the exertion, I stood bent over at the waist for a minute to catch my breath, then disposed of my slain enemy. I then took a quick, well deserved bath to freshen up and put the house back in order before the guests returned from the beach. I had just resumed preparing lesson plans when the beach crowd returned, reporting a wonderful afternoon of swimming and eating delicious grilled fish with rice. They quickly inquired about the status of their sick friend. That stumped me since I had completely forgotten about her in the fray.

"I think she's fine," I reported, "I haven't heard a peep out of her. Feeling a bit guilty, I added, "I wanted to let her rest."

A couple of the women went in the master bedroom to see about her and found her sitting up, rubbing her head.

"Are you alright?" they asked, feeling her forehead to see if she was still feverish.

"Yeah, I think so," she answered drearily, "But I think my fever got really high earlier! So high that I was hallucinating! "

"Hallucinating!!" they exclaimed, in unison. "What did you see?"

She sighed wearily, explaining,

"Well, it wasn't what I saw. It's what I heard. I thought I was being attacked by some kind of beast. I heard panting and grunting, thrashing sounds, like something was running, and things falling. I was really terrified."

Looks of sympathy and horror reflected on her friends' faces as they gasped,

"Oh, how scary! Perhaps we should take you to the hospital."

"No, no, I feel better now," she said, shaking her head. "That was awhile ago. I'm beginning to feel hungry now. That's probably a good sign, don't you think?"

All three ladies emerged from the bedroom, and recounted the harrowing tale of the hallucination, holding the others' rapt attention. I listened intently, immediately recognizing the probable source of her hallucination, but remained very quiet.

"Wow," the computer programmer said, "that must have been a dangerously high fever. Are you sure we shouldn't take you to the hospital?"

"Or perhaps it was some wicked spiritual warfare attack," another piped up, which received serious nods of consideration and concern.

"Well, let's let her get something in her system first," I interjected cheerfully, "then we'll see how she feels. She seems to be doing better already. Sometimes we just have to get past the point where the fever breaks. Shall we all have snacks as you recount the joys of your afternoon?"

I headed to the kitchen to make some popcorn while toying with the idea of letting our gracious guests return to the States with a tale of supernatural encounters, but couldn't bear to let the deception continue. So I confessed my heroic battle against the humongous, attacking moth the next day, much to the recovering woman's relief and her friends' delight. I could hear my old friend Lisa's words echoing,

"Oh, I wish I had a camera."

Lessons for the Traveler:

1. Best to shut doors before sunset to avoid an onslaught of light seeking creatures.

2. There are better ways to return a flying insect to its natural habitat than going towards it with a broom.

3. In the absence of extenuating circumstances, hallucination inducing fevers warrant a trip to the emergency room.

48

Creative Solutions

The average Indonesian's ability to come up with effective, if unconventional, solutions to problems, never ceases to amaze me. One time, I moved into a building that was designed for a business on the first floor and living space on the second and third. Unfortunately, my sixfoot square mattress was too large to fit up the narrow stairs. The worker who was putting up a plywood wall to section off a room told me he could solve the problem if I was willing to "open it." The worker was be my good friend's older brother, so I had a good rapport with him and felt confident in his judgement and ability. I thought for a minute, wondering what he meant to open, but then deferred to my general trust that Indonesian people are master problem solvers, so I gave him the go ahead to "open it."

The next thing I knew, my friend's brother was using a sledge hammer to knock out the cement stairs and ceiling that were impeding the progress of the mattress! It was a new building and the noise brought a crowd of gawkers from the surrounding buildings as well as passersby on the road. I was frozen with panic! He was knocking out the walls! After several minutes and several square feet of rubble piled on the floor, he took a moment to wipe his forehead and noticed me standing in the doorway, frozen with my mouth gaping open, covered by both hands, unable to voice a sound or even blink.

"Don't worry, I'll fix it back. You'll see," He explained, calmly, with an encouraging smile on his cement dust covered face. "I have cement and paint here with me. The important thing is that we get your bed upstairs, right?"

Speechless, I tried to smile back and nodded in agreement. The cookies had already crumbled, milk spilled, there was no point in arguing otherwise. Sure enough, within three hours, the mattress was in place, and the cement ceiling and stairs restored. He returned the next day to repaint the repaired openings, and no one could tell what had happened because his work was better than the original workers'. I saw no need to mention the future removal of the mattress because I knew he could simply "open it" again.

Lessons for the Traveler:

1. Savvy Indonesians know how to solve problems in ways that wouldn't occur to average Westerners.

2. Be open to unconventional solutions to perplexing problems.

3. If the meaning of an expression if unclear, best to ask for further explanation.

49

My Unlikely Bodyguard

Part of being a community oriented versus individual oriented society means avoiding conflict for the sake of just one person. There are times, however, when a conflict is unavoidable, even for just one. While I was living in the big city, a friend from a city without a mall asked me to search for a bathing suit for her ten year old daughter. I didn't know much about shopping, children, or clothes, let alone shopping for children's clothes, so I asked Ita's mother to accompany me to the mall.

When we arrived at the mall, Ita's mother led me to a nice department store. While we were searching through the various racks of bathing suits, a young woman in her late teens asked me, in English, if we needed help. She had an English dictionary in her hand, so I supposed she was wandering through the mall, striking up conversations with foreigners to practice her English. I chatted with her about our search for the bathing suit, and about her siblings and hobbies, etc. Finally, we selected a bathing suit and went to the cash register to pay. When I pulled out my wallet, she said,

"Would you give me money?"

"Excuse me?"

"Will you give me money?"

"I'm sorry, no. But I sure enjoyed visiting with you. Your English is quite good. I wish you well with your studies."

"I need money. I'm hungry," she persisted.

"Oh, if you're hungry," I said, "Come with us and we'll eat together here in the mall. That will be fine."

"Uh, no, I need money because my father's in jail. Don't you want to help me? I need money for school."

She was clean and dressed nicely, so I wasn't sure what to think as she continued,

"We don't know what happened to my father. He ran away and my mother doesn't have money. You can give me money."

Her comments were becoming random, so I determined she either wasn't all there mentally, or she was simply saying whatever she could think of in English. Ita's mother and the salesclerk couldn't speak English, so they thought we were just enjoying a pleasant conversation. They looked on, smiling, clearly impressed with the young woman's English skills.

"I'm sorry. I need to go now. Have a good day."

I turned to Ita's mother and asked if she was ready to go. We started out the door with the young woman glued to my elbow, continuing to ask for money with increasingly outlandish tales. I stopped and said to the young woman,

"If you are hungry, we can get something to eat right now. Otherwise, I'm going to shop some more, but I don't need you to accompany me, okay? You have a nice day."

She just looked at me.

"Are you hungry," I asked again.

She shook her head no, and drifted back a few yards. When I created some distance between the the young woman and us, I told Ita's mother than the young woman concerned me because she was saying strange things, and that I feared she would follow us.

"What? Her?" Ita's mother said, "No, I'm sure she is just an English student excited to meet a foreigner and practice her English."

"Well, whatever you say. I'm just saying she gives me the willies."

"She's just a young girl, and she's obviously smart because her English was perfect."

I don't know how Ita's mother felt qualified to judge the girl's skill level when she didn't speak a word of English herself, but it was true that the young woman didn't stumble over her words. Just as we turned into the bookstore, I noticed the young woman following us.

"Aha!" I whispered, "See? She's following us. I knew it. That girl makes me uncomfortable."

"Maybe she's just looking for books like you are. This is a public place. Stop being so sensitive. She won't bother you," Ita's mother retorted, rolling her eyes.

Sure enough, I breezed through the English materials section when, in the corner of my eye, I saw the young woman approaching. I went over to the agricultural section, and she followed me there, too.

"You can give me money? I don't have any parents and nowhere to live."

"I'm so sorry," I said, "The offer for a meal is still open, but if you don't want to eat with us, then I'd like for you to leave me alone so I can look for books in peace."

"I need the money for books. Will you give me money?" came the response.

I could feel my temper beginning to rise, so I excused myself and hurried back over to Ita's mother in the magazine section.

"Let's leave here. That girl won't leave me alone," I reported.

She looked around to see the girl lingering three shelves over, waiting to see my next move.

"Oh, ya?" Ita's mother said, beginning to get the picture. "Alright, we'll begin to walk down the mall, and if she follows us, I'll speak to her."

"Okay, but don't make her upset. I don't think she's mentally stable," I warned.

So we began our jaunt down the mall corridor and the young woman followed us. In a very casual voice, Ita's mother said to me,

"Bi, you keep walking. I'll catch up with you."

I knew Ita's mother was going to solve our problem, but I couldn't imagine how. I kept walking, slowly, but kept close enough so I could hear what happened. Ita's mother went straight for the jugular,

"Hey! Are you following us? We don't want to be followed."

I didn't hear the girl's response, but she must have denied following us because Ita's mother continued,

"I SAID, we DON'T want to be FOLLOWED! Do you understand? Do you want me to slap you?!"

Problem solved. The young woman shook her head "No" and headed the other way.

Ita's mother sauntered up to me as if nothing happened and asked,

"Ok, Bi, where do you want to eat?"

Ita's mother, my hero, all 5'2 of her!

Lessons for the Traveler:

1. Deciphering when to give money to people who request it is a difficult matter. Trying to meet a real need is better than handing out cash.

2. There's no shame in having an Indonesian friend help in uncomfortable situations. More often than not they can communicate more clearly than you can.

3. With age comes authority in Indonesian society, so grandmothers have more power than you'd suspect.

50

Initial Re Entry
After the Tsunami

On Jan 5th, 2005, I re entered my beloved province, in the wake of one of the most devastating natural disasters recorded in human history, the tsunami. Many of my friends had rushed out of the province, seeking refuge from the havoc and chaos enveloping the province, the ravaged coastal regions in particular. I was scheduled to ride shotgun in a newly purchased black pickup truck packed to the brim with various survival supplies to be distributed in the heavily damaged capital city of Banda Aceh. The plan was for me to catch a ride up the eastern coast with an Indonesian friend who had been in Banda Aceh the morning of the tsunami, but had brought his wife and son out of the province to stay with relatives until things became more stable. He and his family had lived in my old apartment after the civil conflict had caused me to relocate the 18 months prior to the tsunami, so I was not worried about taking such a long journey with him. Besides, I knew we would stop halfway to Banda Aceh and have lunch in my old hometown,

Lhokseumawe, with my friend Ita.

My phone rang before dark the morning we were supposed to leave. My friend's father had been admitted to the hospital, so he wasn't free to drive up the coast with me. The packed truck was in my driveway, so I determined I would see what I could do about finding another driver. I suppose I could have driven myself, but it seemed unwise to travel so far alone. Ita's stepfather was a well known and respected bus driver for one of the major bus lines running from Banda Aceh all the way to Jakarta and back, and their terminal was within a mile of my house, so I drove the packed pickup to the bus terminal, and got out to find some help.

Immediately, the men working at the terminal recognized me as Ita's stepfather's "adopted daughter," so they greeted me and informed me that he was still in Banda Aceh, but safe and well. I told the group of men that I needed one person who was willing to drive me to Banda Aceh, and that I'd pay him a handsome fee, plus bus fare for the return trip. The men looked at each other, then to the ground, and no one said a word until one petite young man stepped forward and said,

"I'll take you."

"Do you have a legitimate driver's license?" I asked. "May I see it?"

He got it out and handed it to me. He couldn't have weighed 110 lbs nor stood above 5 feet tall, but he was not intimidated by me. I looked at him and thought for a moment, "What's the worst thing that could happen?" I could see he wasn't armed, and I doubted he would try to overpower me. We'd be riding with the windows down, so it would be too noisy to talk much, and I could call for help immediately if needed. I knew the way to Banda Aceh, too, so I would know if he tried to take me somewhere else. I would drop him off at the bus terminal in Banda Aceh and drive to my friend's house myself, so he wouldn't know where I was staying nor anyone I knew. Plus, everyone there saw him and knew that I was part of Ita's family, so if anything happened to me, they'd make him pay. More than anything, I knew Ita would have lunch on the table in six hours, and I planned to be there.

"Can you leave right now, in this truck?" I asked him directly, trying to maintain a professional distance.

I was looking for a driver for the day, not a boyfriend.

"Yes, let me go get a clean shirt for tomorrow. I'll be right back."

While he was gone, I asked the men if they knew him and where he lived. They said they did know him and his mother, too, so I felt like he wouldn't try anything questionable. The community accountability in Indonesia would work in my favor. Ten minutes later, we pulled out of the station and headed North. We chatted just enough to be sociable on the way to Ita's, and I made a point to call a few friends on my cell phone to let them know I was on my way. I wanted the man to see that I was no fleeting tourist or journalist, or even disaster relief personnel, but rather a normal person with a strong network of Indonesian family and friends. Ita had prepared a feast for lunch, and invited over some long time friends for a mini reunion.

I wept with Nevi as she told of her own struggle for

survival as the tsunami waves had taken her under three times until finally she and her husband and her mother in law found refuge in a tree they were able to catch as they were carried along. She told of another friend who had become separated from her husband and toddler son in the rushing waters, only to later meet up again with her husband, but no son. He'd been ripped away from her husband's arms, never to be seen again. Awful, tragic stories, but still, thankfulness for each survivor and the chance to carry on.

I could have stayed with Ita for several days, but duty called me to continue the journey with my driver. Ita's husband, Samsul, had taken the driver to the men's area to converse while we women were socializing in the living room. Samsul, not physically much larger than the man, and a driver himself, made sure my driver understood he was carrying a valued family member, not just some foreigner. So, we departed for the second half of the trip with full stomachs and plenty to discuss. I felt safer since he'd seen me in the context of Ita's family. He saw that I had not handed out money or goods there, but had just stopped to spend time with loved ones.

Two hours from Banda Aceh, just before we started up the mountain, the driver shocked me by asking me where *we* were going to sleep.

"Oh, we will go to the terminal, where you will get out and I will pay you the agreed upon amount, and I will drive to my friend's house to stay. Her mother and sisters are expecting me," I answered as if I hadn't understood his intent.

I then turned the conversation to something nebulous

from the morning's newspaper. The driver ignored my suggested topic and began to ask inappropriate questions about why I wasn't married and what type of experiences I'd had. I told him outright that I didn't feel comfortable with that type of talk, that I was a follower of Christ, and committed to a moral, godly lifestyle, and that if he wanted to discuss spiritual matters, that would be fine, but that I would not entertain vulgar speech. He acted as though I was joking or being coy, and told me to loosen up some. On one hand, it's probably not wise to alienate one's driver. On the other hand, I knew I could drive the rest of the way with no problem by myself.

"If you're going to talk that way, just pull into the terminal when we get to Sigli, and I'll give you your fee, and I'll drive the rest of the way by myself."

"Whoa, whoa, alright then," he conceded, and we rode in silence another fifteen minutes. "All I wanted to know was where we were sleeping."

"Where?" I slammed my hands on the dashboard and yelled, "*We* not sleeping anywhere! *You* are going to get out at the terminal, and I am going to my friend's house. I know that many people think American women are immoral, but I'm not, and I AM OFFENDED!"

"Alright! Alright! There's no need to get mad," he stammered.

"Okay, I'm glad we can come to an understanding," I answered, looking straight ahead.

We rode the rest of the way in silence. At the terminal in Banda Aceh, I opened my door almost before the truck completely stopped.

"Here we are," I quipped, "Thank you for bringing me here safely. I appreciate your effort. Here's the money I agreed to pay you, plus your return fare. I hope your life will go well. Goodbye."

"Okay," he said, as he received the money from me.

I drove away, thankful to be in Banda Aceh, in the truck alone, on the way to my friend's house. In retrospect, I was foolish to get in the truck with a stranger. I suppose it was my desperation to re enter my beloved province, along with my disproportionately positive expectations of Indonesians that led me to such an ill advised decision. Still, I only suffered a bit of indignation and no real danger, so I might do it again, in a similar situation. There's just something within me that doesn't want to believe an Indonesian would act with genuine intent to harm me. Is that a bad thing?

Lessons for the Traveler:

1. Beware that conversation a western woman views as chit chat might be viewed as seductive by a local man.

2. Community accountability has many benefits, but there's no substitute for personal caution.

51

A Dangerous Delivery

The evening I arrived in Banda Aceh, I drove directly to
Popi's house. It was wonderful to see them again, but as with
so many reunions, meeting was bittersweet, because Popi's
eldest sister and her daughter were lost in the tsunami.
Almost every family had lost members. Some families had
lost more than remained. One former neighbor, Dek Bit, had
come to my house in Medan and asked me to take canned
goods to her husband in Banda Aceh. He had decided to stay
in their house, cleaning the remains of the tsunami water
stains that had invaded their home. I wasn't surprised by Bang
Mul's diligence, because he had always kept their house,yard,
and car immaculate. I assured Dek Bit I would be glad to
swing by to check on him with a box of food and supplies.
Their house was just a few blocks from Popi's, so I planned
to go the following day.

The day passed quickly, however, as I had many people
I wanted to see. Plus, I picked up my friend Leny Katan, a
loved and respected Chinese Indonesian coworker and
long time friend who came to Banda Aceh to facilitate

disaster relief efforts. Leny and I had done all the ground work to open an English course in Medan in January of 2005. When the tsunami hit Aceh, however, all those plans were set aside, and we turned our attention towards the crisis in Aceh. Leny stayed with me at Popi's house. After the evening prayer time, just after dusk, I mentioned to Leny that I had a delivery to make, just 8 blocks away, and invited her to go with me. I told her it wouldn't take but five minutes.

The roads near Popi's house had been cleaned off fairly well, and the electricity was running at least part of the time at night. As we turned down the street towards Dek Bit's house, however, Leny and I noticed that not only were there no lights, but it was like a ghost town with no sign of a person anywhere. The thick tsunami water residue was still caked on the streets, making it hard to tell exactly where the streets ended and the open sewage gullies began.

"Uh, Alice," Leny said quietly, "I don't think we should go any further. There's no one around and the roads aren't clear. We could get stuck in the mud."

"Oh Leny," I said, "Don't worry. This is my old neighborhood. I know right where to go and it won't take us but a minute. Besides, I told Dek Bit I would deliver the package to Bang Mul and that's exactly what I intend to do."

"But Alice, if we get stuck in the mud, there's no one around to help us," Leny protested, the pitch in her voice rising.

"We're not going to get stuck. I know how to drive. Plus, this is a new truck with good tread, so we'll be fine. You'll see," I encouraged.

I could see that the conditions were less than ideal, but I

honestly thought, "How hard could it be?"

"Alice, I don't like this at all. It smells like dead people. There could be corpses in the mud. Let's go back. We can try again tomorrow, or meet him somewhere to give him the food."

"Oh, for crying out loud, Leny," I scolded, "Don't be a baby! We're just going to drop this stuff off and go right back to Popi's. Quit worrying!"

I could feel by the way the truck was handling that the mud was getting deeper, but I was resolved to give make the delivery as I'd promised, so I just tightened my grip on the steering wheel and reminded myself that we weren't going far. I couldn't imagine putting the truck in reverse and trying to get back out, so I just kept going, knowing the road was a big circle and would let us out back on the cleaner road, if we could just get through. Leny tried not to nag, but her tension and my own growing tension, filled the truck.

We could feel the truck sliding left and right beneath us. I rolled forward slowly in the dark, in the silence, wondering how Bang Mul got through this terrible mess everyday. The stench in the air was a mixture of rotting flesh and grime from the bottom of the ocean combined with churned up waste from the open sewers lining the roads throughout the neighborhood. The houses in the neighborhood had minimal damage, but the roads were nearly impassable. I only needed to make two turns to lead us back to safety. As I approached the first one, which was quite sharp, almost a U turn, Leny could hold her silence no longer.

"Alice, be careful. Do NOT go into the gutter. Can you see? The mud's so thick. Be *careful*," she moaned.

As always in moments of fear, I began to chant my state the opposite mantra in a calm voice, to reassure myself more than Leny.

"No one's afraid here. We're going to be alright. Slowly, slowly, make the turn..."

"Alice, we're sliding!" Leny shrieked. "Stop the car! Don't go in the gutter!"

"Okay, we're sliding a bit," I practically whispered, throat parched, "but no one's worried here. We got it, we got it... no one's sliding into the gutter..."

"Alice, NO ONE is here! Bang Mul is NOT in his house and there are no lights on at all, not even a candle! Oh, there are probably spirits of dead people all over the place here..." Leny whimpered.

Just then, the car lurched forward, and I couldn't stop it. It slid out of control, in slow motion, off the road. I slipped the car into reverse, and the wheels spun in the mud. I couldn't think, consumed with panic. Leny fell silent. She couldn't even mouth the words, the truth of our condition, that our front wheels were in the gutter.

"Leny, I just want to say before you say anything that I was wrong and you were right. You have every right to be upset. I should have listened to you and I didn't, and I'm so terribly sorry. Okay, let's pray," I continued, without waiting for Leny's response.

Leny couldn't make a sound and was nearly comatose with fear. I might have heard a little whimper, but it was hard to hear anything over my pounding heart.

"Lord, I was a fool to come here at night. Leny tried to tell me, and I wouldn't listen, but she was right. Lord, I acted stupidly and You don't owe me a rescue here because I got myself into this, but, Lord, if there's any way, please, please help us get out of here."

With that, I put the truck in reverse, and gunned the engine, terrified it would send me into the gutter behind me, but not knowing what else to do. We popped right out of the gutter and found ourselves back in the street.

"Oh, Thank you! Thank you!" I exclaimed.

Slowly, but with increased confidence because of the Lord's clear favor toward us, I turned back towards the direction from which we had come.

"We're almost there, Leny. We're going to be alright. I'm so sorry I did that, Leny. I shouldn't have done that."

I just kept prattling on to Leny's silence. Finally, by the Grace of God, our wheels rolled onto the cleared off part of the street where we could get real traction again.

"Ha! See? We're okay! We made it. It's behind us now, Leny. We're going to be alright. I promise I'll never do anything like that to you again. Please forgive me."

"Alice, just shut up!" Leny screamed, "I am *so mad* at you right now!" she cried with a cathartic sob. "You never listen to me! You put me in danger back there, you know? And you say you'll never do it again, but you will! You're so hard headed sometimes!"

"Leny, you're right. You have every right to me mad at me. I was wrong. I'm so sorry. I don't know what else to say except, well, let's just be glad we're okay, alright? Nothing bad happened to us."

"Don't talk to me! I cannot talk to you right now! Just take me back to Popi's!"

"Yes, okay. That's exactly what I'll do."

When we returned to Popi's, I called Bang Mul on his cell phone to apologize for not bringing the food.

"You didn't try to go all the way to the house, did you?" he asked.

"Well, yes. Isn't that where you are?"

"During the day, yes, but nobody in their right mind would want to stay there at night. There's still no electricity and none of the neighbors have returned. Plus, it smells like death. I only go by during the day when the hot sun hardens the mud enough to pass safely."

"Oh, that's wise," I mumbled.

We agreed to meet in a more accessible area the following morning for me to give him the box his wife had sent. Leny forgave me, being the lovely woman that she is, but I learned a lesson that day about trying to be a hero beyond all common sense.

Lessons for the Traveler:

1. Even new tires on new trucks have trouble advancing through thick, wet mud.

2. God's mercy is immeasurable, but we shouldn't presume on His favor by being foolish.

3. If a friend is genuinely afraid, that's reason enough to change course.

52

Leny and the Needle

In the wake of the tsunami, countless medical teams rushed in to be of service. The humanitarian aid organization Leny and I worked for facilitated many such teams. We rented an enormous house with nine bedrooms and five bathrooms to house the hundreds of volunteers that would come through during the two years following the tsunami. Leny helped us settle the contract on the house, then returned to Medan to secure supplies needed to run such a large operation. When she returned to Aceh, we already had a medical team on the ground. I picked Leny up from the airport late in the afternoon, and we arrived at the house just as the evening logistics meeting was about to begin.

As Leny greeted the volunteers, one kind nurse noticed that Leny had an ace bandage around her left wrist and asked her about it. Leny described the way she'd sprained it while vigorously cleaning her house three weeks before, and mentioned that yes, it was still stiff and painful sometimes. The nurse offered her some ibuprofen for the pain and swelling, which Leny received with a smile as she headed upstairs to settle in. The rest of us took our places for the meeting. Every evening, we needed to determine the next day's personnel distribution and transportation assignments.

Several minutes into the meeting, I heard Leny calling my name in soft, sing song fashion, so as to not disturb anyone else.

"Alice? Could you come up here for a moment please?"

"Be right there," I answered, remembering that this was Leny's first visit to the house since we'd set it up as our headquarters and figuring she must have had some questions about where to put her stuff. When I turned the corner into the women's bedroom, Leny was standing with her back to me.

"Here I am, Leny. What can I do for you?"

"Alice," she said, turning to face me, "The lady with the curly hair downstairs gave me some medicine for my wrist and I think I'm having an allergic reaction to it. Look, my face is swollen and I'm having trouble breathing."

Sure enough, her face was bloated to the point her eyes were almost shut! Panic shot through me as I heard the words, 'I'm having trouble breathing,' but I didn't want to scare Leny any further, so I simply quipped,

"Okay, let me go get her," and scurried down the steps as fast as I could.

The nurse was sitting on the bottom step, so I sat on the step behind her, leaned over her shoulder, and whispered,

"Leny's upstairs, perhaps having an allergic reaction to the medicine you gave her, because her face is swollen and she's having trouble breathing."

The nurse whirled around, eyes wide open, and gasped,

"She can't breathe?!"

Before I could answer, the nurse called out to the other medical people in the room,

"Emergency! Leny can't breathe!"

All seven medical personnel jumped to their feet, grabbed their equipment, and dashed up the stairs in a blur. The main doctor took the lead and told the nurses to lay Leny down on the bed. One nurse took Leny's vital signs while another spoke calmly to her and another stroked her hair. The nurse taking the vital signs then stirred in her box of medical supplies to find an IV needle because Leny needed medicine, and fast. Our only Indonesian medical person present was a veterinarian, so he stood back, watching carefully. With all the commotion, I just sat next to Leny, looking on. Leny was very cooperative until it came time for the needle.

"Oh, Alice," Leny said desperately, "I don't like needles! I don't think all this is necessary. If they just give me an antihistamine, I'll be fine. No needles!"

The doctor assured her it was better to be safe than sorry, so the nurse continued searching through in her box, lamenting the fact that she couldn't find an appropriate needle.

"Leny, these people are professional and they're going to help you. Just remain calm," I encouraged.

"Well, this will have to do" sighed the nurse holding up a needle. And she proceeded to probe Leny's arm with it.

"Noooo!" hollered Leny, "No needles! Ouch! Ouch! Alice, make her stop!" Leny cried.

I had always felt so much love and respect for Leny, I couldn't believe she was freaking out like that, to the point of tears.

"Leny, they're helping you. Okay, so it hurts a bit, but you need it. Just hang on, Leny, you'll be alright."

"OW!! It hurts!" she screamed, "Take it out!" Leny's gross overreaction to a little needle stick was truly mystifying.

"Leny, come on now, settle down. It'll just be a minute," I semi scolded, at which Leny covered her face.

Finally, Leny's vital signs improved and her swelling went down enough for her to breathe normally again. The emergency handled, the nurse removed the IV and the medical team returned downstairs to continue their logistics meeting. As they were filing out, Leny examined her face in the mirror, through damp eyes, still caressing her punctured arm. It wasn't long before the explanation for Leny's extreme reaction became abundantly clear. The veterinarian sided up to me and said, in typical understated Asian fashion,

"You know, I was very surprised to see them stick that needle in Leny's arm. I wouldn't have used a needle that size for anything smaller than a horse."

Lessons for the Traveler:

1. If a well respected person is behaving out of character, there's probably a good reason for it.

2. Not all needles are created equal. Horse and human needles should be kept in separate places.

3. Don't be hasty to judge another's reaction to pain.

53

Exploding Organs
and Satellite Phones

I used to be quick to dismiss the use of connections to get
unusual help as cheating, the antics of the rich and arrogant.
I wondered why we couldn't just get along the best we could
like normal people, rather than calling on special privileges
for ourselves simply because we could? One evening,
however, just two months after the tsunami when the city was
still in disarray, I learned just how precious a little
connection could be. I had just come into my little room,
waiting my turn for an evening bath, when the guest house
coordinator came in flustered. She told me I must rush one
of our volunteers to the emergency room because he had
severe pain in his abdomen.

I thought our best option was to take him to the Danish
healthcare center since the regular hospital historically hadn't
been one's best bet to receive satisfactory medical care. So, I
took the grimacing volunteer to the clinic set up on the
college campus nearby. I jumped out to ask for assistance,
addressing the first person I saw.

"Hello, my friend is in terrible pain. Can you help him?"

"Oh, I'm sorry, Miss," said the Danish man, "We're orthopedic doctors. It looks like your friend needs to go to the emergency room at the general hospital."

"You mean the regular hospital?! Have you *ever* heard of anybody getting help there?" I blurted out without thinking.

At this, a wave of shame swept over me because I loved the local people and I knew there were fine doctors around because I'd had some as students in my English classes. (Of course, some those very students had told me that if I ever needed serious medical attention, I should rush to Medan or better yet, to Singapore). Anyway, Danish doctor responded,

"Well, there are American doctors in the emergency room."

"Ah, now that's a different story," I sighed with relief, turning to help the volunteer, now doubled in pain, back into the car.

And off we rushed to the regular general hospital's emergency room. When we arrived, I was delighted to find that one of my former students was on call. She took us in right away to a gurney near a table with several people sitting behind it. An American nurse came around the corner, and began to examine the volunteer. She and another doctor decided after some prodding that my friend needed to have his appendix removed. Hearing that, my gallant friend muffled an expletive which, in all fairness, seemed justified in this dire situation. The Tennessee man (yes, our volunteer was a Tennessee volunteer, no joke) then piped up,

"I want to go to the USS MERCY," which was a hospital

ship just off the coast of the city. It was at that point, a Reggae singer looking doctor with about 100 braids, and a degree from a fine university in the U.S., stood up from behind the table and announced,

"You're not going to the USS Mercy! They only do certain kinds of procedures, and that don't qualify!"

At that announcement, Lord forgive me, I muffled a few expletives of my own rushing through my thoughts. Dr. Reggae came over to examine the patient himself and declared that, yes, it did seem that the appendix was "fixin' to explode." With every ounce of courage in him, the Tennessee man looked up at the American doctor and asked if he could perform the surgery.

"Well, I would," came the reply, "But I've been here since 7 this morning and I got to go!"

"Oh! It's 7:00," interjected the American nurse, "Let me get my purse!"

So she ran to the back and reappeared with her purse to leave with the American doctor. But as she headed out the door, she called back to us,

"There's a fine Australian doctor in surgery now, but I've told him you're out here. He'll get to you next. Goodnight!"

And they were gone, our countrymen... The Indonesian nurse noticed the ailing volunteer's dismay, so she invited us to move his gurney to an area less crowded while we waited for the Australian doctor. We were ushered around the corner to one of only two empty gurneys in the emergency room. On the other side of the narrow passageway from our volunteer's gurney, an Indonesian woman, about 40 years old, was lying on a gurney, waiting to be seen, too. I determined

I would help comfort him by turning his mind off his own pain by talking about hers.

"I wonder what's wrong with that lady over there," I said, facing him.

I didn't give him a chance to answer before I whirled around to face her and asked in Indonesian,

"What's the matter, Ma'am?"

"I can't move my legs," she said.

"Oh have mercy!" I said back to him, "She can't move her legs! I wonder if it's because of the tsunami!"

Again, turning back to her, I asked

"Is it because of the tsunami?"

"No..."

"No, not because of the tsunami" I translated back to him as she continued.

"I was pregnant,"

"She was pregnant..."

"And I had to have an operation," she added.

"And she had to have an oper... Never mind! That's a dumb story! That doesn't have anything to do with you!" I said, desperate to change the topic.

The volunteer's eyes grew as wide as saucers,

"She came in to have baby and now she's LAME?!" he yelled.

Just then, the Australian doctor appeared around the corner. Perfect timing! He examined the patient and declared,

"Oh, yes, this appendix is inflamed, alright. You'll need to have it out as soon as possible."

Sighing with relief, the Tennessee man said,

"Well, I guess you'll do the surgery."

"I'd like to," he replied, "but I'm afraid I'm not too keen to do it because I've been here all day, I'm tired, and it's 8:00, time for me to go. But there's a world class Indonesian doctor in the back who is more than capable to handle your problem."

Just then, the rest of the volunteer's teammates came in, which included a man who had once been the Chief of Staff at a hospital in the States. He took one look around at the cats running through the emergency room, and listened to the man with the concussion holler out, and he announced,

"These premises are unsatisfactory for my friend to have surgery."

I just gaped at him, wondering what options he thought we had? We surely couldn't put the man on an overnight bus to the big city 12 hours away. No flights were available until the following day, and the USS Mercy didn't do "these kind of procedures," so we'd been told. The Australian doctor reiterated that if he were in the Tennessee man's shoes, he would let the Indonesian doctor remove his appendix. I was satisfied by that solution, but the Tennessee medical team members deemed the conditions unacceptable. While I was waiting for them to realize that we had no choice but to have the operation there, one of the Tennessee gentleman whipped out a satellite phone and told his wife to get in touch with the Senator of Tennessee who happened to be the Speaker of the House and this man's personal friend!

I stood there dumbfounded, thinking how *that* was the friend to have in a pinch! We took the patient back to the guest house and received a phone call within thirty minutes.

"This is the captain of the USS MERCY. How can I be

of service to you?"

Early the next morning, the man with the satellite phone accompanied his friend on a helicopter to the USS MERCY, where he underwent a successful operation. After the patient had healed sufficiently to fly home, his teammates sent him home ahead of the rest. I later overheard the man with the Satellite phone say that if he hadn't been able to contact the Senator, he would have called Laura... Laura Bush, that is.

Lessons for the Traveler:

1. Some times it pays to have friends in high places.

2. For the record, there are many competent Indonesian doctors who perform successful operations every day.

54

Swapping Favors

After the tsunami, medical teams from all over the world came to Aceh in droves, bringing higher quality medical professionals and equipment than the province had ever seen. And all that care was FREE! As a result, every person with an ailment throughout the province, affected by the tsunami or not, rushed to Banda Aceh to see medical attention. Hordes of people crowded the main hospital from morning until night, every day, for months. I was working alongside volunteer medical teams as a translator/driver when I wasn't serving in the education sector.

One day, we were working in a coastal village that lost more than 80% of its population to the tsunami. Two women needed immediate care, so I was tasked to take them to the hospital and get them in to see a doctor. That day, I did *not* think "How hard can it be?" because I knew it would be a nightmare fighting the masses. Sure, I had friends who worked at the hospital, but they weren't in charge during this chaotic season, and I couldn't imagine how I would find them even if they were.

No, we'd just be three among the sea of people clamoring for attention at the hospital. I know the ladies in my care hoped I would use my clout as a foreigner to push them ahead of the crowd, but I didn't feel right about that. Some of those people had been in line since early morning. So, I told them we'd get a number and wait like everyone else.

We waited for hours. One thing exacerbating the chaos was that the sound system was broken in the little building where they were calling out the names of the next patients to be seen. So the hordes would press up against the glass, desperately asking,

"Who did they call? Who did they call?"

The people closest to the front would try to help by yelling out the names into the crowd, but between the sheer volume of patients, and the various states of infirmity, it was total pandemonium. It occurred to me that a bull horn, or a simple set of speakers with a microphone would do wonders to help. When I could no longer resist using my foreign face to seek special favor, I went around the back of the building and boldly opened the door, which surprised the haggard registration personnel inside. I know they thought, "Oh no, some foreigner's here to complain or make demands."

"Good afternoon," I greeted them cheerfully, "I have been here for several hours with two ladies from the village. If you call them within the next thirty seconds, I will buy you a new sound system while they're talking to the doctor. I can bring it here within thirty minutes."

Amidst the stunned silence, someone braved,

"Could you throw in a couple of fans?"

"You got it! And some water. The ladies names are..."

Those officials couldn't find my ladies' cards fast enough! They scrounged through the piles and came up with them in twenty seconds.

"Okay, thank you. We've got a deal!"

So I gathered up the cards and escorted my ladies to their respective doctors. I told them to wait for me on a certain bench, that I'd be back in a few minutes. I then dashed to the market, where I bought two big active speakers, a microphone, and three stand up fans. When I returned, lugging the goods into the back door, the staff cheered.

"You did it! You came back," they exclaimed, as if surprised.

"A deal's a deal. Thanks for your help. Here's your water. Have a good day," I called as I rushed back out the door to pick up my ladies.

How joy filled my heart when, as the ladies and I were passing by the registration building on the way out, we heard names booming across the courtyard. Such a simple solution, and not very expensive, either. Why hadn't I thought of it sooner?

Lessons for the Traveler:

1. Using clout as a foreigner is a sensitive issue. Try not to use it unless you can provide benefit for local people, too.

2. One silver lining of the tsunami was the high quality, free medical care provided for more than two years by compassionate people from all over the world.

3. There are often simple solutions to confounding problems right before our eyes. Be on the lookout for ways to help.

55

Three Special Guests

Three months after the tsunami, we got word that three special guests were coming: the wife of the president of our company, her sister, and the vice president's wife. They were planning to work alongside us for three weeks! Although I knew and loved the top tier wives, I thought to myself, "We don't have time to entertain poopahs right now." I picked them up at the airport and was delighted to see them, all splendid women with delightful personalities. But I had a ladies' luncheon in my old neighborhood that afternoon, so I offered to drop the honored visitors off at the guest house to get settled in.

"Well, I'd like to attend the luncheon myself," piped up the president's wife, turning to the other two, "How about you?"

"Oh, that will be fun," chimed in the vice president's wife.

"I'm with y'all," added the president's wife's sister, in her classic Mississippi drawl.

In my heart, I wondered *how* I would be able to visit with my old neighbors since I'd need to translate for these three women, but I had forgotten a vital piece of information. Both of the top tier wives had lived in Indonesia, though many years ago, so they didn't need a translator. Sure enough, the moment we arrived, the president's wife broke off to the right and the vice president's wife off to the left, and they commenced mingling with other guests at the luncheon.

The first lady's sister stayed with me and was a terrific sport about trying the food and letting me visit with friends. My old neighbors were highly impressed that I'd brought guests from America who could speak their language. Plus, my guests had the much honored grandmother status, so as a matter of protocol, the hostess of the luncheon invited the ladies to speak a few words to the group. "What a sweet gesture of respect," I thought, sure they would decline. I couldn't imagine that either of the women would be prepared to make a speech in Indonesian after at least a decade, perhaps two, out of the country. I was mistaken.

When the hostess opened the floor, asking it they would like to say a few words, the president's wife responded,

"I believe I would."

The ladies in the room whispered with delight, but I sat silent, stunned. What would she say? Our first lady gave a brief, but eloquent speech telling the ladies of her sorrow over their loss. She assured them of God's love for them and for their province; that He had a plan for them, so not to lose hope. She closed with the words,

"And I believe my friend would like to say a few words, too."

Another murmured wave of approval swept through the room, all eyes turning to the vice president's wife.

"Yes, I would, thank you," she answered, competent and lovely in her own right. She spoke a few words of greeting and comfort, then began to softly sing, "God is So Good," in Indonesian, with the president's wife joining right in. My big bosses' wives were singing at the ladies' luncheon in my old neighborhood, how surreal! The local women received their compassionate words warmly and thanked them profusely for coming, inviting them to attend future meetings when they were in town. What a start!

Several days later after working with us shoulder to shoulder in various disaster relief efforts, the president's wife expressed sympathy for families that had to live in tents because their homes had been washed away.

"I wonder what it would be like to sleep in a tent," she said wistfully.

Uh oh, I knew what that meant... So, we made arrangements to spend the night in a village on the coast that had only a fraction of survivors after their entire village had been swept away. Only the bottom half of the mosque remained. I didn't know much about camping, but I'd always assumed that when erecting a tent, all rocks and debris were first removed from the ground underneath. Such had not been the case for our tent, so lying on the thin bamboo mats that night was far from comfortable. Our honored guest got ready for bed by using little silver clips to pin her perfect hair into place, and she put moisturizer on her face as part of her nightly beauty regimen. I made a mental note that night to begin applying moisturizer nightly because her skin was still fresh and wrinkle free.

So, we chatted with an Indonesian woman from our team

who had accompanied us, and a little girl who came in our tent with us, and we laid down for a restless night. Just before the break of dawn, the speaker on the mosque blared out the morning call to prayer. Without a moment's delay, the president's wife sat straight up on her mat and declared in her sweet Southern drawl,

"Isn't this fun?! I'm having SUCH a good time!"

And she appeared to mean it! I thought to myself, "My back hurts," but said nothing except,

"Good morning."

I marveled as I watched her release the clips from her hair to have her bangs fall right back into their perfectly coiffed position. She had those beauty tricks down to a science. We enjoyed many other adventures with our three wonderful guests. Their genuine example of servant leadership, humility, flexibility, and compassion for the people truly challenged and inspired me. They had come with no thought of being entertained nor impressed. They just wanted to encourage us and contribute meaningfully to the work; and that's exactly what they did.

The day before they left the province, we had another serious tsunami warning. I'll never forget their perfect poise as we deliberated whether to join the masses of people fleeing inland or take our chances remaining where we were. We discussed being sure everyone had access to large flotation devices in case the water overtook our house. We stood on the balcony watching long lines of headlights desperately trying to escape from coastal areas. I thought to myself it would be a terrible shame to lose these three champions along with us, but if it were our time to go, I couldn't go in better company.

Lessons for the Traveler:

1. Nothing inspires like a good example to follow.

2. Genuine servant leaders are rare, and to be cherished.

3. To live and work, and if called upon, die, amongst kindred spirits, is a great privilege.

56

Escorting Brides

I attended countless weddings during my time in
Indonesia: sang at a few, acted as the photographer a time or
two, even washed dishes, but only once did I have the
privilege of escorting the bride to the door of her groom's
house for the ceremony. It all started when my friend asked if
I could make my car available for use to escort her relative to
the party at the groom's house. I was glad to be of service, so
I took my car to the car wash the morning of the party and
showed up at the bride's house as promised just before 10:00.
Her house wasn't more than a mile off the main road, but I
found myself deep in the village, among people who stared
and marveled to see a foreigner dressed in traditional clothes.

   When it was time to load the car, I was surprised to see
the fully adorned bride pop into the front seat, next to me,
rather than ease into the back seat like I'd seen other brides
do. Several of her cousins and aunts piled into the back, and
we made our way to the groom's house, which was only two
neighborhoods over. When we arrived, I parked the car on
the dirt road about twenty yards from the groom's front door.

I sprang out of the car and was ready to walk towards the house when I noticed the bride was still in the car. I thought she must not understand how to open the door, because she just sat there. I dutifully walked around the car and opened it for her, smiling broadly.

"Well, come on, girl. This is your big day!"

When she still didn't get out, I realized there was a protocol problem. The female leader of the village was supposed to hold a special yellow umbrella with sequins and strings of beads dangling from its edges over the bride's head as she exited the vehicle. Together, they were to walk to the gate of the groom's house, where she would then release the bride to the groom's people. We waited for ten minutes in the sweltering heat, but no one came to the bride's assistance. I finally asked,

"Where's the village leader lady? Shouldn't she be here to hold the umbrella for you, Honey?"

She thought for a minute, then thrust the umbrella into my hand.

"YOU do it, instead!" she ordered.

Shocked that I would be in such an important cultural position for a girl I didn't even know, I stood frozen for a moment. Then I shrugged with a grin,

"Well, alright. Let's go!"

After all, how hard could it be? So, I opened the decorative umbrella, helped her out of the car, and began the promenade towards the groom's house. Naturally, jaws dropped open to see me escorting her, but no one offered to take my place, so we strolled on. As people called out to me, I didn't want to appear arrogant, so I smiled, nodded, and waved hello to the children like I did everywhere else. Unfortunately, in my vigor to be friendly, I became a bit negligent with the umbrella, such that it bobbed down too far and got stuck in one of the flowery, antennae like prongs bouncing gaily above the bride's poofed hair. I didn't notice what had happened until I heard her cry out,

"Hey! Hey! The umbrella! It's caught!"

OOPS! That poor girl. She had to be thinking, "All the cool foreigners in the world and I get a total geek! I hope this isn't a bad omen for my marriage!"

Thankfully, I didn't end up lifting her headpiece entirely off her head and flinging it into the bushes. We were able to get it unstuck without even stopping the procession. Without further ado, I handed her off to the groom's mother, who received her with a different open umbrella at the gate in the front yard. My role completed, I was able to enjoy the party with the other guests. I did resolve, however, that should I get another such opportunity, I would try to be more attentive to my duties.

Lessons for the Traveler:

1. When involved in official ceremonies, best to pay attention.

2. Try to be available and helpful whenever possible.

3. Hanging beads are best kept out of close proximity to bouncing antennae.

57

Watching Puddles

In the tropical heat, rain often came as a pleasant relief. With rain, however, came potential hazards, and I once ran smack into one during the highest celebration of the Islamic year, Lebaran. Coming at the close of the fasting month, Lebaran is a joyous season of donning new clothes and visiting friends and relatives, tasting myriad delicious treats in each house. I often picked up friends during the first few days so we could visit others' houses together.

One afternoon, I picked up my friend Popi to begin making the rounds. As we drove along, I got caught up in our conversation such that I didn't notice two things ahead of us: a large puddle of standing water from the morning's shower, and a woman wearing a lovely purple ensemble walking along the side of the road. Popi and I were laughing about some silly tale when we heard SPLASH! The puddle was so deep that when we hit it, half of the windshield got soaked. Unfortunately, and completely without forethought or malice, I also drenched the lady in purple. I didn't realize it until I saw her fussing at me in the rearview mirror when I ran the windshield wipers to clear the front and back windows. Seeing me wince as I looked back, Popi immediately turned around in her seat to assess the damage.

"Alice!" she gasped, "You splashed that lady!"

"Yes, I see that, Popi. I didn't mean to. I'm so sorry. I didn't notice the puddle because we were talking. Do you think we should go back?"

Popi didn't answer. She just hunched down in her seat and muttered,

"You should pay more attention when you're driving, you know. That's really bad, splashing someone like that. She's going to have to go home and change now, and those were probably her new holiday clothes."

That wasn't the first time I had been scolded for not paying attention while driving, but it was the first time I took it seriously. From that day forward, though I still had a propensity to multi task while driving, I really did keep an eye out for potentially hazardous puddles on the road.

Several months later, I was chatting over lunch with a friend who was working on her PhD in Kuala Lumpur, Malaysia. I asked her about cultural differences, if there were things that she had trouble adjusting to even after living there for several years.

"Well there is one thing that still upsets me," she confessed. "When it's raining, and you're standing on the side of the road waiting for a bus, cars and taxis don't make any attempt to avoid puddles. Here in Indonesia, we try to be considerate of pedestrians, but there, they seem to get a thrill out of splashing us. I can't tell you how many times I've have to go home and change clothes. It's so rude! Can you imagine?"

Awkward silence, blink, blink. My glazed over eyes wandered to her half empty glass next to her plate,

"That sounds awful... more tea?"

Lessons for the Traveler:

1. Puddles on the road seem harmless to people in cars, but they can create big messes for motorcycle riders and pedestrians. Be aware of splashing others.

2. The *community first* mentality in Indonesia carries with it many blessings for individuals, like consideration for pedestrians.

3. If you are the pedestrian, best to give puddles a wide berth just in case another foreigner drives by.

58

Healthy Perspective

My favorite form of exercise in Indonesia was riding a bicycle. On my bike, I felt close to the community, smiling and waving while passing on my way to run errands. When I needed more air in my tires, I would pull over to one of the many makeshift air fill and tire repair stations sprinkled along the side of the road. Eager to head off any comment about the condition of the bike, I usually beat the person to the punch with a line like,

"My tires need air, probably because of the great burden they must bear (tee hee)."

But one afternoon, I was taken aback by the response I received to that comment. The 60 something man tending the station yanked the cord to start the air compressor and walked right over to chide me.

"You have a big, strong, healthy body," he said gently, but firmly, "You should be glad you are able to ride your bike all over town like you do. There's nothing wrong with your size."

I just stared at him for a moment, wondering if he were an angel in disguise. The one place I had always felt open to criticism was my size. But this unique man affirmed me, and he was right. What kind of fool wouldn't be thankful for a body healthy enough to ride a bicycle for miles at a time? After a lifetime of grieving, hiding, and apologizing for my broad shoulders, I saw them with a new perspective. Anyone passing by would have seen a haggard old man adding air to the tires of a foreign woman's bicycle tires. No one would have guessed that he was speaking wise, healing words that the woman would never forget.

Lessons for the Traveler:

1. Never take a healthy body for granted.

2. Be alert to wisdom coming from unexpected sources.

3. Affirming words are best remembered; hurtful words forgotten.

59

On Being Stylish

I've never cared about fashion. As far as I was concerned, if I wore clean clothes that covered my body, I was doing alright. It suited me as a child for Mom to order clothes from the Sears & Roebuck Catalog, or just bring something home for me to wear. I had no knowledge of nor concern about brand names or current fashion trends. Through the years, that never changed. I bopped along for decades in ignorant bliss. After the tsunami, I hit the jackpot with volunteers who came over for two weeks, donning modest clothes that they wouldn't be inclined to wear back in the States. They left the unwanted clothes with our guest house coordinator, who then offered them to me. Where else would I get clothes big enough for me, and *free*, at that? Anything she offered me that fit, I was glad to absorb into my wardrobe. After three years, I had quite a collection of shirts and blouses.

One day, however, it was time for a reality check, and one of my Indonesian friends, Deb, was the one to give it to me. We were close friends, and Deb was known for her gentle, but to the point speech, so she was the perfect one to address me. We had already established an open rapport as in days by she had commented on my hair.

"I saw the pictures of you when you were little and you had the sweetest little white blond hair. But how did it become so dark? Now, it's the color of…rat fur."

Now, I'm not an overly sensitive person about such matters, but I had to object to that one. I turned to my friend, and said,

"Deb, I know I have low standards, but never, ever, use the words *rat fur* to describe the color of a woman's hair."

She agreed to toss that phrase from her vocabulary, but when she asked me a phrase I could use to more accurately describe the present color of my hair, I couldn't think of one. But I digress... I was visiting Deb in Medan one day, when she launched into *the talk*,

"Kak, (older sister) it's about your wardrobe… it's *got* to change. You need to stay away from button up shirts. You already look masculine enough with your big body and short hair, but those look like men's shirts."

I wasn't the least bit offended because I trusted Deb and knew she was trying to help me.

"Oh? The buttons should be on the right side to be women's shirts," I reasoned, "Don't you think they're all the same? I'll be big in whatever kind of shirt I wear. Besides, I got these for free, you know," I said proudly.

"Yes, I can tell," she dead panned. "Okay, you're still big, but you could wear more feminine clothes. The outfits you wear when you teach are becoming, like women's clothes, but these striped button up shirts have to go."

"You think so? They're still good, though. They don't

have holes or stains."

"I know, but that's not the issue," she persisted, "They aren't attractive. Go get some material and have some feminine clothes made."

"How will I know what's pretty? I am oblivious to such things, you know. Everything looks alike to me. As long as it's clean and modest, I don't care about the style or color."

"Precisely. That's the problem. Take Melissa with you. She's stylish."

Melissa was a fresh college graduate from my alma mater, and, come to think of it, she did always look sharp. So I agreed to ask Melissa for assistance upon my return to the province. As luck would have it, my young stylish friend picked me up from the airport, so I was able to explain my predicament and ask for her guidance. She stifled giggles, embarrassed on my behalf as I recounted the conversation with Deb, and beamed when she heard her own name suggested as the person to lead my wardrobe make over.

"I'd be delighted to help you! I know exactly what to do! This is my area of expertise, you know," she grinned.

We arranged a material shopping trip as our first step in the process. Melissa knew my horror of shopping in congested traditional markets, and especially for clothes, so she was very merciful.

"We'll just go through the shops to get a feel for what's here and might be suitable for you. No need to feel pressure to buy anything, let's just see what kinds of textures and patterns you find attractive."

Under Melissa's tutelage, I felt secure to begin the foreboding task... and I indeed found myself drawn to certain bolts of material. Perhaps the influence of my extended stay in the rural area revealed itself as my eyes were drawn to patterns and colors I'd seen my older Indonesian friends wear with aplomb.

"What about this one," I proffered.

Paragon of patience and self control, Melissa said light heartedly,

"Okay, let's stay away from the large prints and horizontal stripes…"

"What do you think of this one? This one's pretty."

Melissa turned from some materials she was examining to reply,

"Yes, that *is* pretty…if you're a granny in the village."

Oh, I was so glad I had Melissa with me, because I can't imagine what I would have come away with if not. She steered me from the polyesters to the cottons, from the loud prints to the tasteful, from the bold colors to the soft, pretty ones. In most cases, I deferred to Melissa's judgement because I could see she really did know what she was talking about. This was not new territory to her. After two or three hot and tedious hours, we arose from the market with six cuts of beautiful material for shirts, and two cuts for pants. I thanked Melissa profusely and told her I'd take it from there.

"I'll go see the seamstress, Cut, and have her make some nice feminine blouses for me."

"Have you thought about potential styles?" Melissa queried.

"Styles? Well, Deb told me a basic shirt with no buttons up the front would look nice."

"Yes, for one, maybe two. But what about the others?"

"Oh, it's okay if they're all the same. Or maybe Cut will have ideas. It doesn't matter. I've already taken enough of your time."

"Are you kidding? This has been *so* fun for me!" Melissa assured, "I'd really like to go with you to see Cut."

"No, absolutely not. Look at your flushed cheeks from the heat. I need to take you home so you can cool off. You've already worked hard enough."

"Actually, I have something I need to talk about with Cut myself, so I need to go anyway... "

I knew Melissa's wicked ways. She didn't trust me. She had taken on the mantle of responsibility for a wardrobe make over and she didn't want me to wreck it. I saw she was determined, and secretly felt thankful she was willing to go, so I agreed to go together. When we arrived at the seamstress's, Cut immediately exclaimed,

"Oh, what lovely material! Who picked it out—clearly not Alice!"

Just then, my helper's aunt was passing by on her way home from the rice fields and, seeing my motorcycle out front, stopped in.

"Hey, what's going on in here," she called as she came through the back door.

"Alice is getting some new clothes made," Cut answered.

"Well, it's about time!" came the exuberant response. "What are you going to do with your old clothes," she asked, turning to me.

I suspected that she was hoping to score them for herself to wear in the rice fields. But first, I wanted to clear up why she'd said it was 'about time' I got new clothes.

"What's wrong with my clothes," I asked, "Give an example of clothes I shouldn't wear. They're all polite."

"Well, take the clothes you're wearing now. They're hideous. You need to throw those in the trash and burn them when you get new clothes from Cut."

Ouch! My clothes didn't even rate for the rice fields! Who knew the whole community had noticed my clothing? Melissa jumped in to give Cut ideas about blouses she thought would be attractive, and they discussed the matter in some detail with minimal intervention from me. Cut measured me to be sure I hadn't changed since the previous round of sewing my teaching outfits, and we set a date for me to pick up my new wardrobe. Ten days later, I went for the fitting alone, and I was thrilled with all of my new duds. My friends were RIGHT, it really did make a difference in my appearance! I made my debut in a new outfit at our Friday afternoon meeting. One of my Asian friends rushed right over to me, all smiles.

"Wow…that shirt looks very nice on you… and it goes with your pants," she cooed.

"Thank you," I beamed, "Melissa helped me pick out all the material and counseled Cut on the styles."

"Oh, very good…" she continued, "When's the last time you bought a new shirt?"

I stumbled for a moment, "You know, I can't remember. I got a lot of new shirts from the volunteers who left them behind, you know. But I can't remember the last time I took initiative to buy something new to wear."

"Yeah," she smiled, with no intent to be critical, "we used to see those same shirts on the laundry line… month after month... just those... "

Everywhere I went around town, almost without exception, my Indonesian friends greeted me saying,

"Oh my gosh! Is that a new blouse?! It looks GREAT on you! You know, I've been meaning to mention that to you for quite some time... "

Evidently the community was just short of sending around a petition about my clothes! Who knew?

Lessons for the Traveler:

1. Sometimes you can unwittingly create a disturbance.

2. Your wardrobe matters to the community more than you realize. Being covered isn't enough.

3. Only your true friends will tell you hard things.

60

Irma and the
Buck Toothed Lady

One day, I was driving to the beach with Ita and Irma, who
was in college. We were passing astonishingly beautiful
landscapes of rice fields and low mountains, when we came
across a most unusual sight on the side of the road. There
stood a scrawny, shriveled lady with her two front teeth
sticking far beyond her lips, pointing opposite directions. I
said nothing, but Irma saw me notice her.

"You were looking at that lady, weren't you, Bi?" Irma
asked.

"Yes, I was," I answered, matter of factly, "And do you
know what I was thinking?"

Leaning forward in anticipation of a humorous
comment on the woman's appearance, eyes gleaming with a
hint of mischief, Irma took the bait,

"What?"

"I was thinking, 'She's probably married and has four
children; but I've never even had a proposal!" (Which, for the
record, was not technically true because I'd had several,

almost every time I'd taken public transportation.)

Irma squealed with glee, burst out laughing, and exclaimed,

"Yes! That's RIGHT, Bi!" with what was, above delight, relief.

In her heart, though there was an undeniable comic element in the way that woman looked, Irma would have been disappointed if I had made fun of her. She wouldn't have been the only one.

Lessons for the Traveler:

1. Many boundaries of basic decency transcend race and creed.

2. Best to be on one's toes for character pop tests from the younger generation. They're looking for good examples.

62

Faithful Wounds

There's a verse in the Bible that says, "Faithful are the wounds of a friend." My Texan friend, Jo, has long been one of my most faithful friends because she tells me the truth even when it hurts. Jo and I had been friends in the States before we found ourselves working for the same company on the other side of the world. I had arrived before she had, and lived in a rural setting, so I fancied myself an expert on acclimating to the culture. Whenever I had to go to the capital for visa runs, I would stay in her high rise apartment.

One afternoon, we were talking about various aspects of fitting in with our Indonesian friends, and I got on my high horse about spoiled, arrogant foreigners insisting on the comforts of home, thereby distancing themselves from the common people. I was going on and on, listing examples, and getting more irate with each word, until I was just bursting with self righteousness. My old friend watched me carry on in such an unseemly manner, then said,

"You know, Alice, it's not that what you are saying is not true. But the way you are packaging it, *no* one would want to receive it."

My first instinct was to say that proved my point, unteachable spirits of arrogant foreigners. But I hesitated just long enough to repeat to myself what Jo had said, and let the wisdom of it sink in. I've always championed *truth* above all else, including my own feelings or the feelings of others, but my attitude in this case was effectively blocking out the truth, making it incomprehensible, even undesirable. Jo's words, truer than anything I'd said, pierced my heart. I'll forever be thankful to Jo for the faithful wound she inflicted on me that day. I was reminded about the patience and kindness with which my Indonesian friends had counseled me and guided me to live well in the culture. Could I not show at least that same compassion for my fellow foreigners? Transitions, especially cross cultural transitions, are never simple or problem free. It's all a process that must be handled with care.

Lessons for the Traveler:

1. Don't be too hard on yourself when making transition.

2. Be merciful towards other foreigners in transition, too.

3. When there *are* lessons to share, package them in a way others can receive them.

LaVergne, TN USA
24 August 2010
194475LV00004B/1/P

9 780984 108756